"First Lincoln the President, next Lincoln the Movie, now Lincoln the Proclamation. Whether he's winning Civil Wars or mere Oscars, the man in the stove-pipe hat has his finger on the pulse and this book, art'n'all, transports ol'Abe into the uncharted territory of the new century."

¶ *SIMON WARNER*, author of *Text and Drugs and Rock'n'Roll: The Beats and Rock Culture.*

"THE EMANCIPATION PROCLAMATION and BEING CIVIL, two great works of art exceptionally intertwined!"

¶ *DELFEAYO MARSALIS*, musician, producer, and educator whose current project is the appropriately named *The Last Southern Gentlemen Tour.*

"A subversive take on what freedom means, and it surely does not mean nothing left to lose."

¶ *JIM SAMPAS*, executive producer of the feature film *Big Sur*, and producer of the compilation album *Esperanza: Songs of Jack Kerouac's Tristessa.*

"Lincoln once said 'folks who have no vices have very few virtues.' As BEING CIVIL satisfies like a bad habit, you should read it and be as virtuous as you want to be."

¶ *KEVIN TOLER*, art director, Boston Symphony Orchestra.

"Lincoln, the poet president, gets the dance re-mix treatment from maestro David Greenberg and it rocks."

¶ *DAVID GREENBERG*, writer, director, actor, professor, stepfather of soul, and of the Philadelphia Greenberg clan; like that pins it down, though it does help place him geographically as a Greenberg wholly different than the author.

Being Civil

comprising a collection of
THE EMANCIPATION PROCLAMATION
(final and preliminary drafts)

&

THE GETTYSBURG ADDRESS

by

A. Lincoln

abstrusions
by
D. Greenberg

[product]

beverly | los angeles | bellagio

ISBN 978-1-300-83999-6

Printed through the mighty and majestic lulu.com

First Edition

This publication is for your use only. No other rights have been granted. If, for some wacked out reason, you want to display these designs somewhere other than in the quiet of your own home, assuming yours is quieter than ours, which is no legal definition by the way, only an observation and a weak one at that since you may have teenagers, or tweeners, or toddlers, and then all bets are off as to the quiet of your own home as those buggers seem to think they rule the roost, which they do with all the love we can give them, though if they, or you, take any of these pages and place them in a public place, or reproduce them, or whatever it is you want to do with them outside of your domicile, quiet or otherwise, post me a letter with all your wishes and desires—about the pages mind you, as I have enough wishes and desires for a cast-full of characters, which should have been the next book, or film script, but instead I'm dicking around with Lincoln's writings and obscuring them as works, hopefully and arguably, of art. Once you figure out what you want to do with these things instead of doing something important with your life—like teaching your kid to ride a bike, or create a desalination plant in Chad out of toothpicks and string—send that letter to me. Affix the right postage, of course, as any additional costs added to this project would make the bottom line dissappear into the maw that is the pile of bills now to my left, and soon to be where my sorrowful head will lie after writing this overly long and legal notice, which will be designed, also by me since it costs a pretty penny to have someone else do it and my pennies are not in a pretty place at all. Basically the pennies are all fictional at the moment. My thoughts are to place this text in a tiny and slightly legible font so that only losers will take the time to read this, but not a bigger loser than the one who has to write it all out. Or should I say, winner? They usually take all, and all I want is to take "all" back from those who took that elusive "all" from me, including my pretty pennies. Besides, calling you a loser will not help the situation, just on the off-chance you want to send me oodles of money in order to reprint my designs on mugs, tee shirts, iPhone cases, underwear... On the front of that envelope—don't forget that postage, mind you—address it to David Greenberg, c/o my publishing and design firm:

[Product] 131 Essex Street, Beverly MA 01915

While I would rather have a legal letter on nice paper to have and to hold—letters are so rare these days to be sure—you can also send your requests to the firm's email address: *sku54@comcast.net*. By the way, I am available for Bar/Bat Mitzvahs, though why anyone would want me to autograph copies of this book, or any book for that matter, in the company of thirteen year olds I have no idea, but to be sure, if that is your request, and you have the cash—no checks please—I'm there. I even have my own yarmulke stashed in the pocket of my my suit jacket from the last few funerals and unveilings. My Dad was one, if you need to know. I forget the others. I know there have been other funerals like my Mother-In-Law's, but she was a Baci, which is Polish for Grandmother. At Polish Catholic funerals you don't need yarmulkes and my memory is not the best these days to remember exactly the last ceremonial event held under Jewish purview other than my niece Izzy Greenberg's bat mitzvah, which was over three years ago. I am sure there was something in between, but for the life of me, what that was I have no idea. As a matter of course, I can do weddings as well, but unlike my Dad & Mom who were Justice Of The Peaces in New Canaan, CT, this wondrous state of MA makes the JP post all political and with such hoo-hah affixed that I never pulled the right strings in order to get my folder at the top of the list—since I would rather poke long hot needles into my eyes instead. But, I can serve Swedish Meatballs with the best of them. I also do great with large hunks of meat, carving them that is, or serving soft drinks with ice. If there's liquor involved, maybe not, as I like to taste the drinks to make sure they will be imbibed correctly with the result that, pretty soon, the drinks are strong as shit and the crowd is noisy as hell. Fights may break out. While the tip jar is pretty full by the end of the night, the profits are eaten up by "breakage." Hence the pile of bills that I now have pushed to the floor in the hopes that the dog thinks they are a plaything and rips them up, littering them like soldiers on the Battlefield of Gettysburg. And you probably thought I would never wind this thing toward the task at hand. It was a slow tack to be sure, made all the more slower by all the Mint Juleps and Philadelphia Fish House Punches I created in order to get into the right historical frame of mind. But now that I am here with you at the end of this rant, let us both take leave of this painfully tiny font, and the equally small, or perhaps smaller, thoughts writ here.

Be

Civil

Contents

The Emancipation Proclamation *(final version)*   *1*

The Emancipation Proclamation *(preliminary draft)*   *29*

The Gettysburg Address   *64*

Readables   *76*

Numbers   *85*

Abstracticatons   *91*

    Decades

    Long endure

    Given

    Gave

    Darkest before

    On a great

First version

The Emancipation Proclamation January 1, 1863,

A Trans= cription

By the President of the United States of America.

A Proc=
ma=
tion.

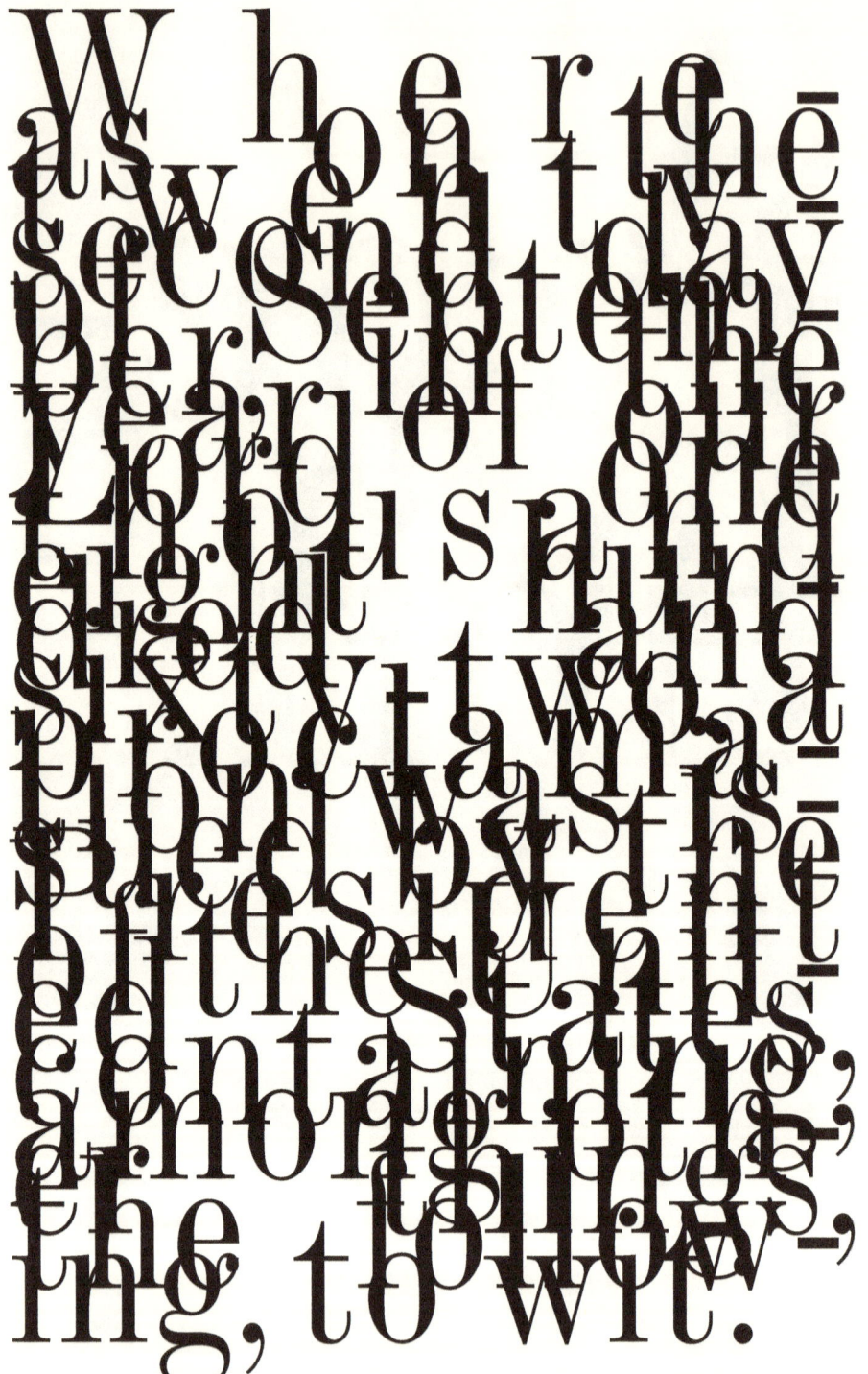

Whereas, on the twenty second day of September, of the year of our Lord one thousand eight hundred and sixty two, a proclamation was issued by the President of the United States, containing, among other things, the following, to wit:

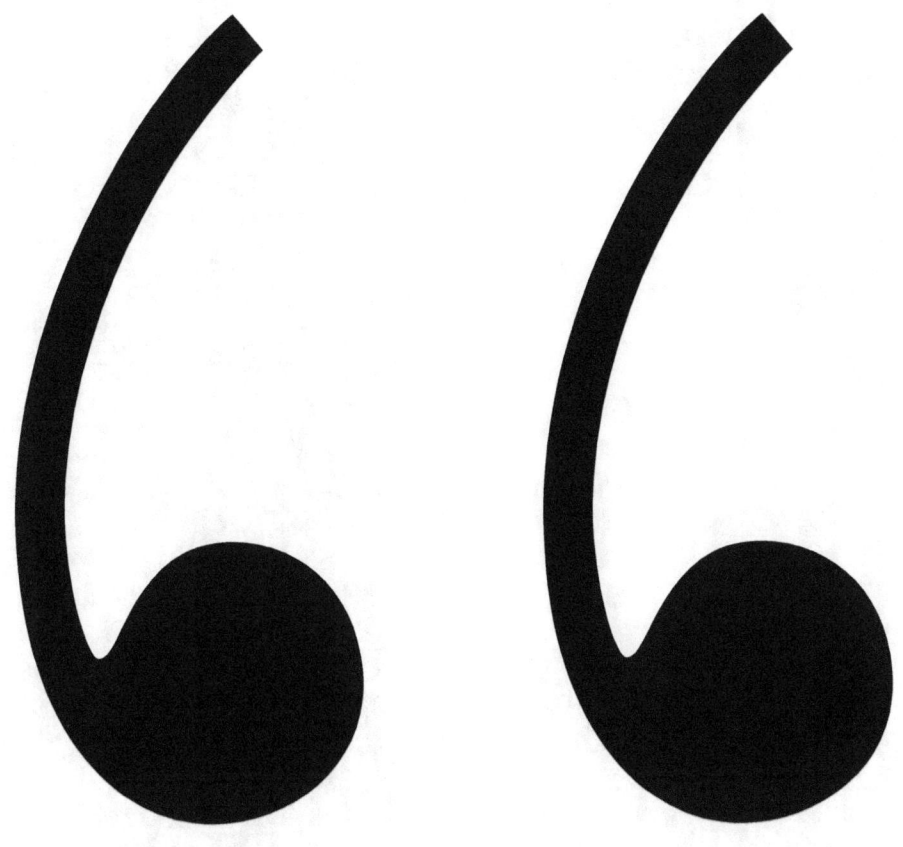

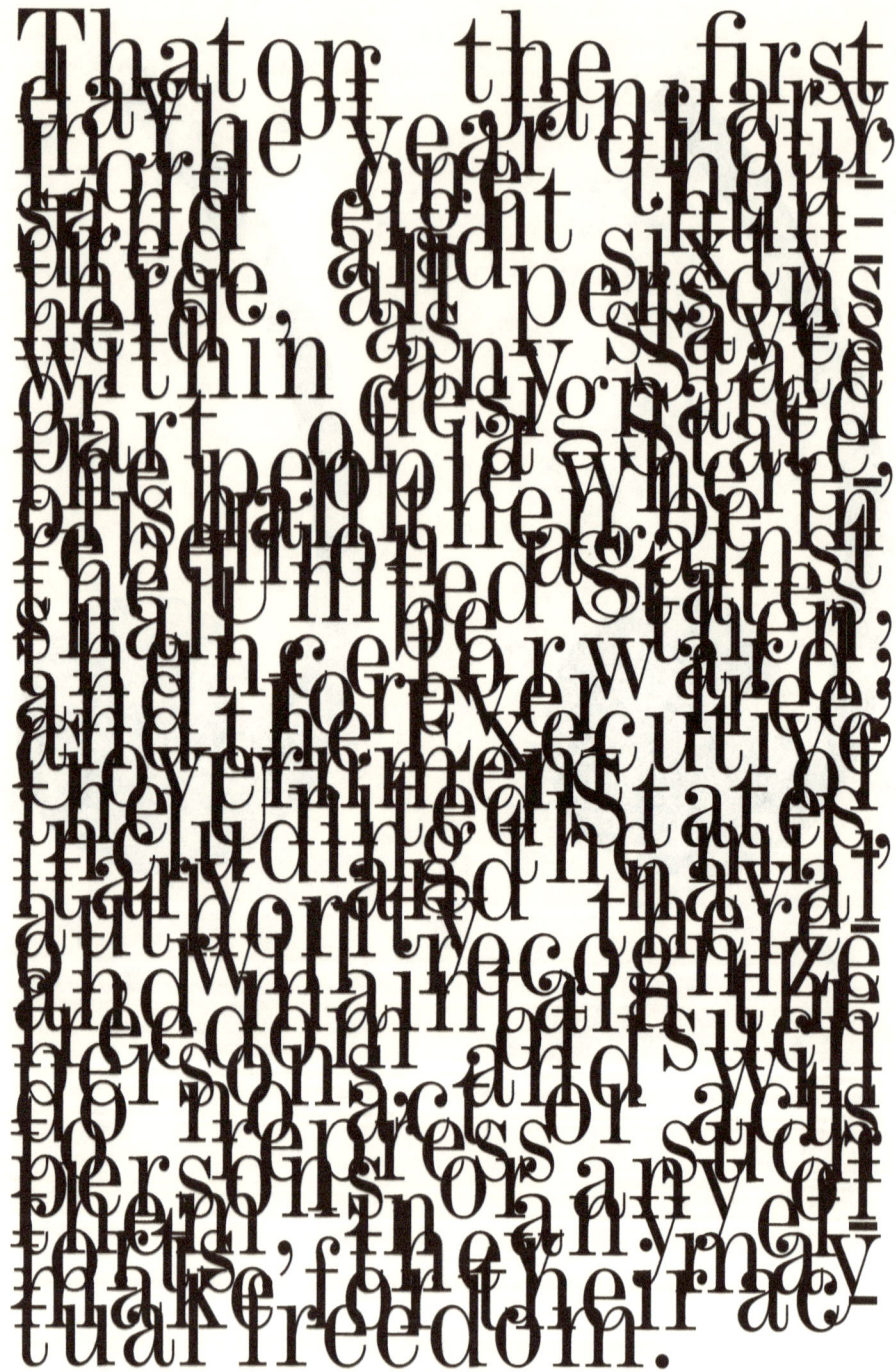

That on the first day of the year of their Lord eight hundred and sixty three, all persons within any state or part of people whereof shall then be in rebellion against the United States shall thenceforward and forever free; and the Executive Government of the United States, including the military and naval authority thereof, will recognize and maintain the freedom of such persons, and will do no act or acts to repress them, or any efforts they may make for their actual freedom.

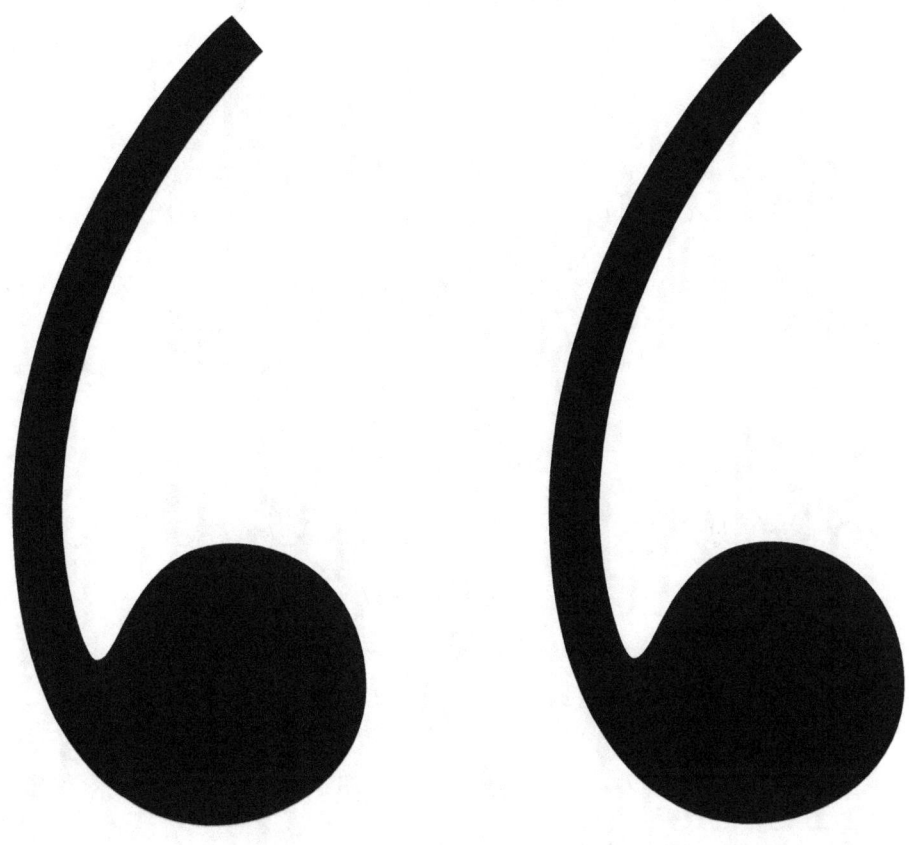

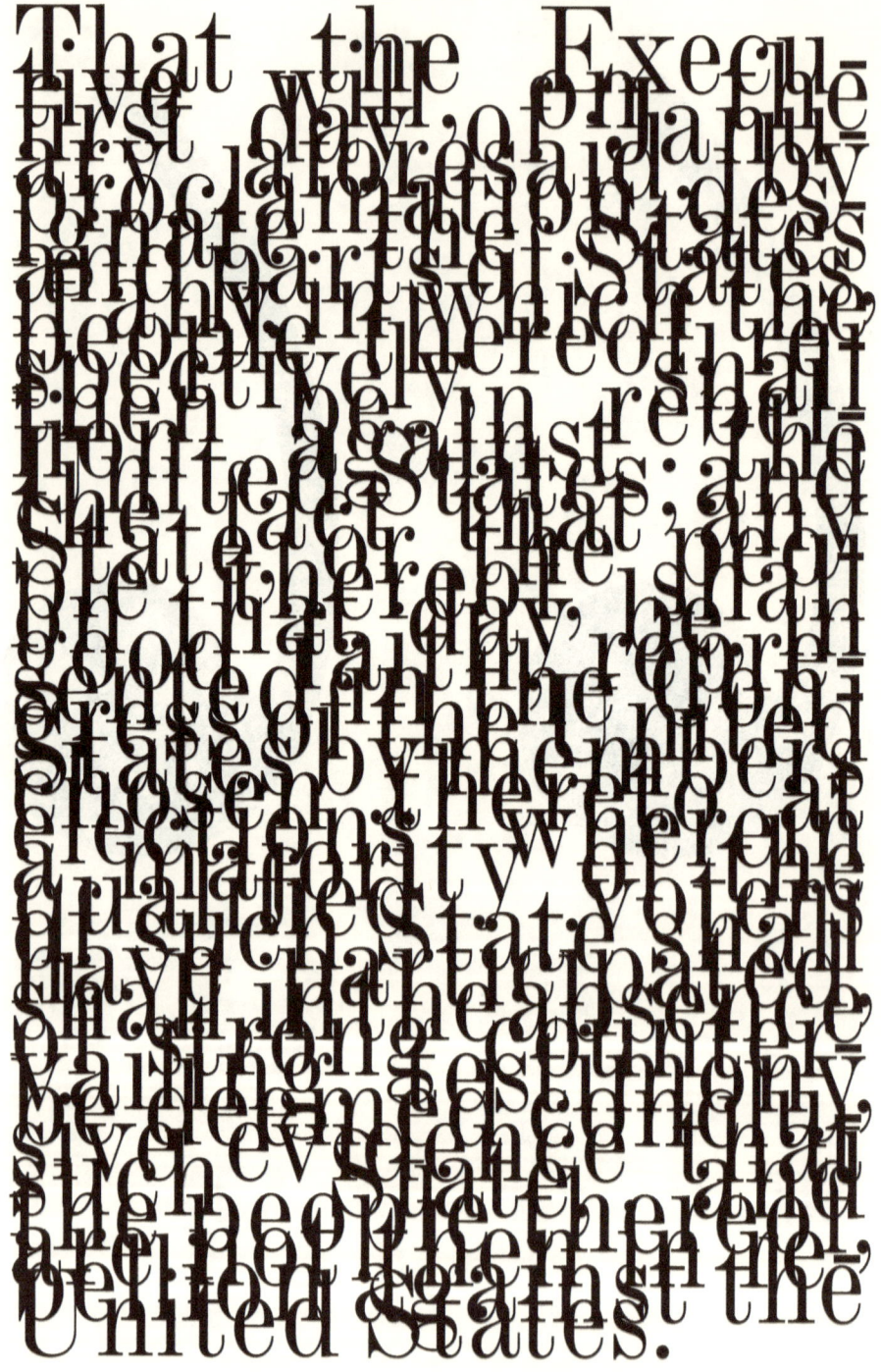

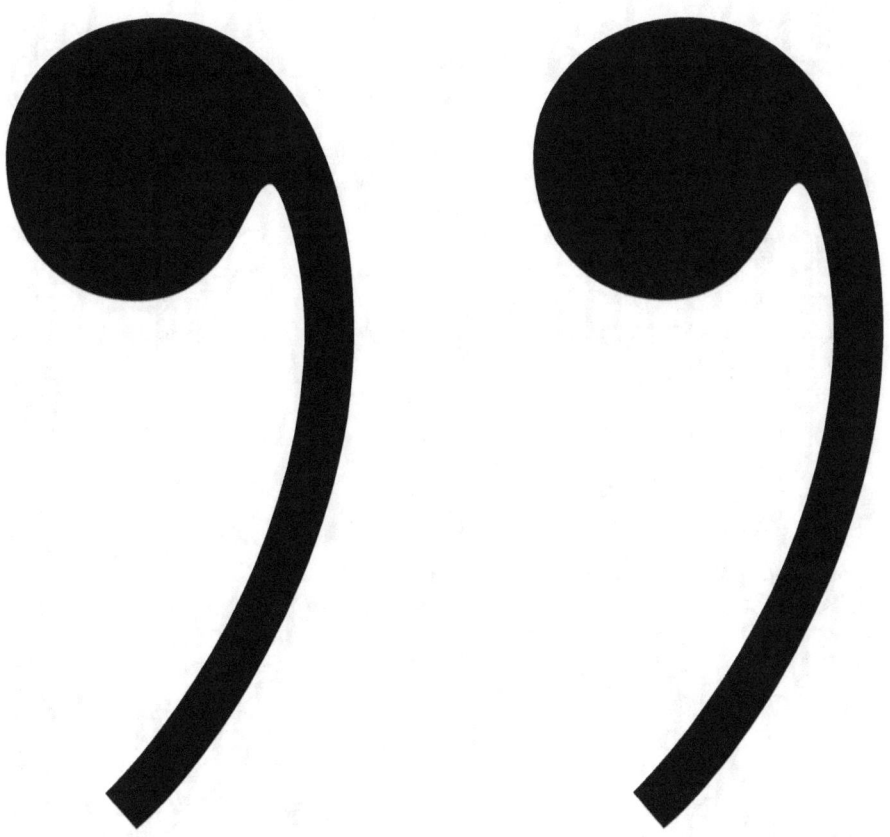

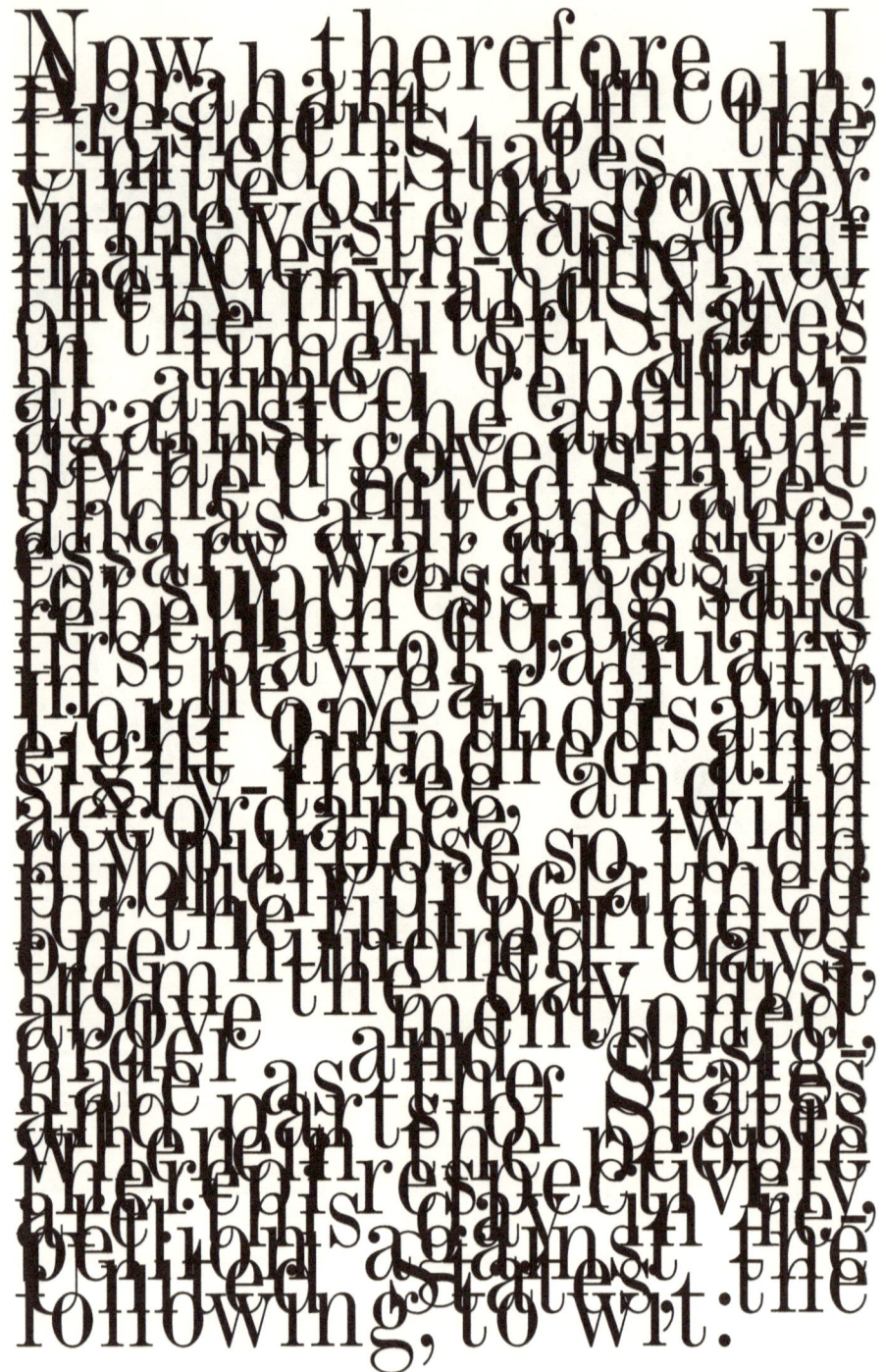

Now, therefore I, Abraham Lincoln, President of the United States, by virtue of the power in me vested as Commander-in-Chief, of the Army and Navy of the United States in time of actual armed rebellion against the authority and government of the United States, and as a fit and necessary war measure for suppressing said rebellion, do, on this first day of January, in the year of our Lord one thousand eight hundred and sixty-three, and in accordance with my purpose so to do publicly proclaimed for the full period of one hundred days, from the day first above mentioned, order and designate as the States and parts of States wherein the people thereof respectively, are this day in rebellion against the United States, the following, to wit:

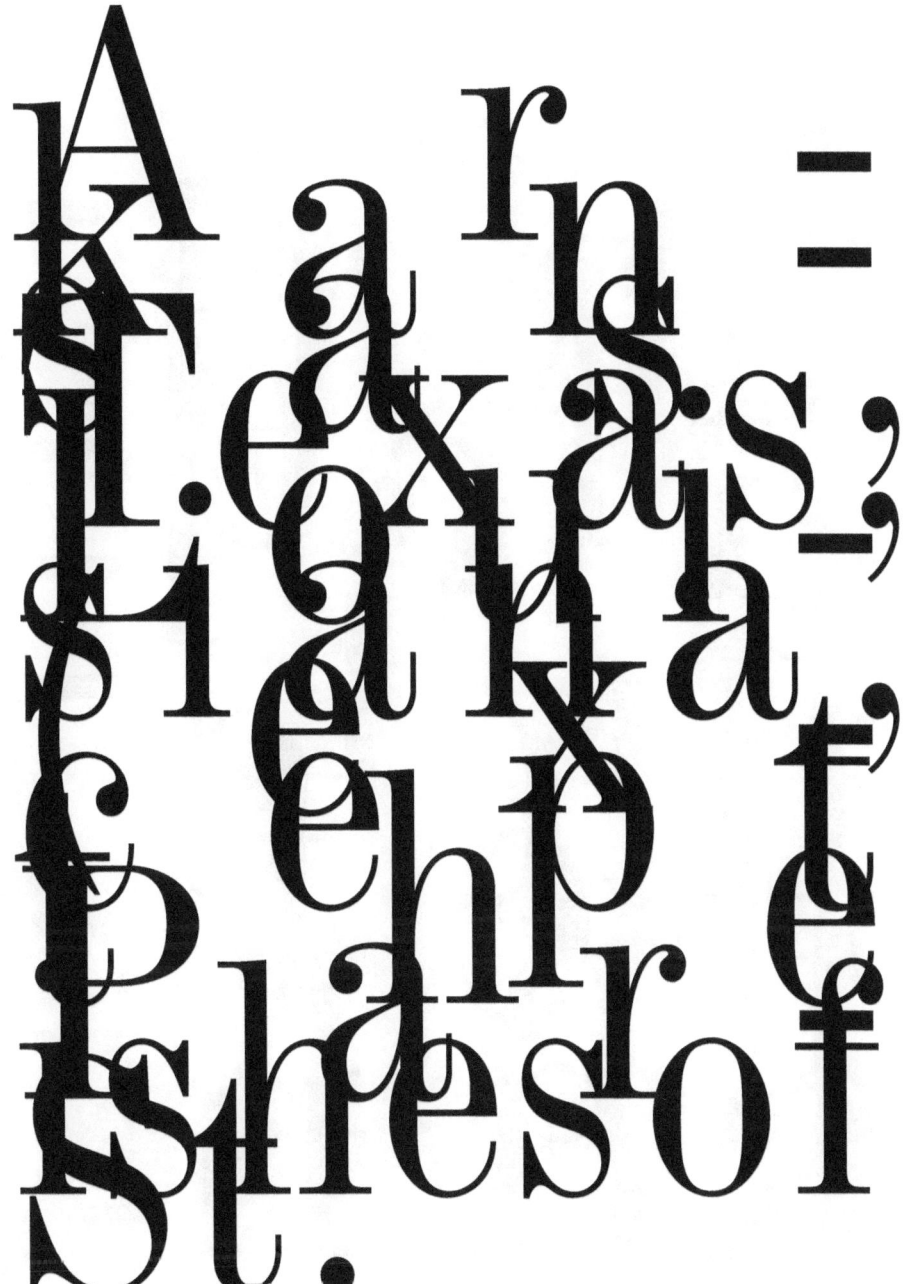

Barnhardtlichtenstein St.,

Jo-nest.,

Char- Char-
St es,
t.

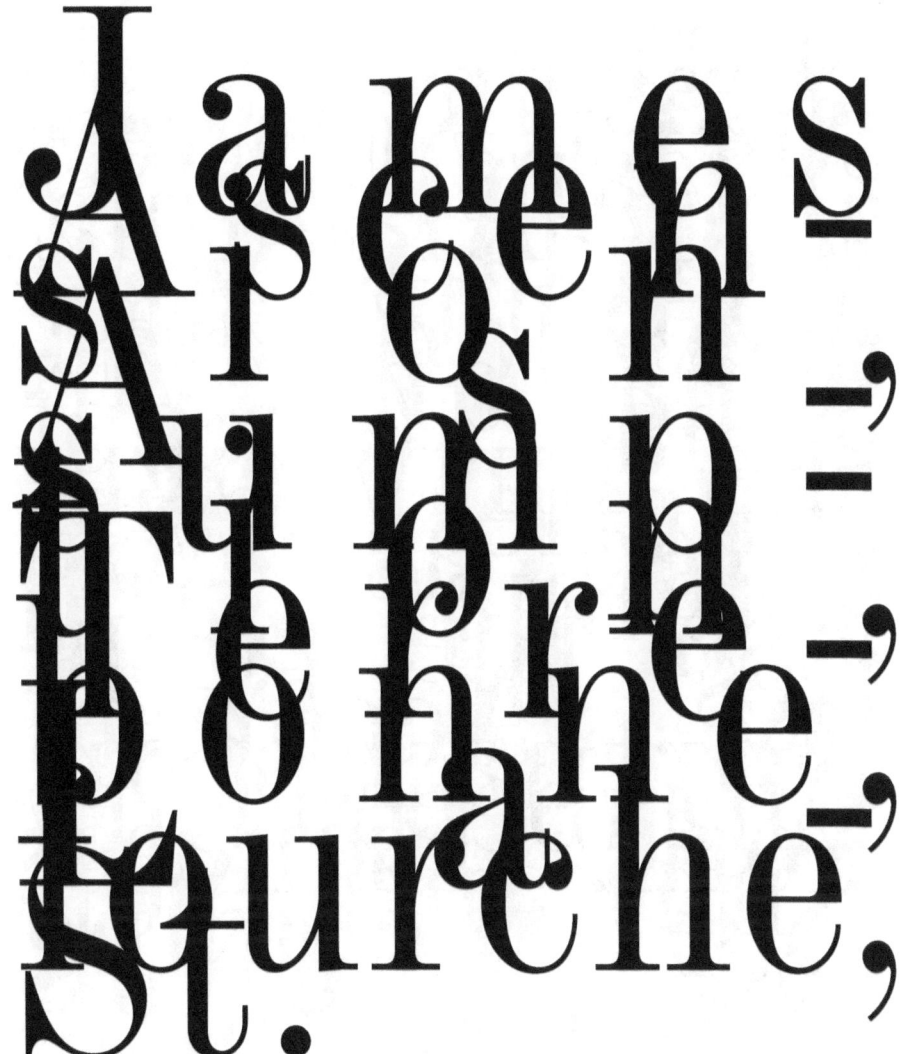

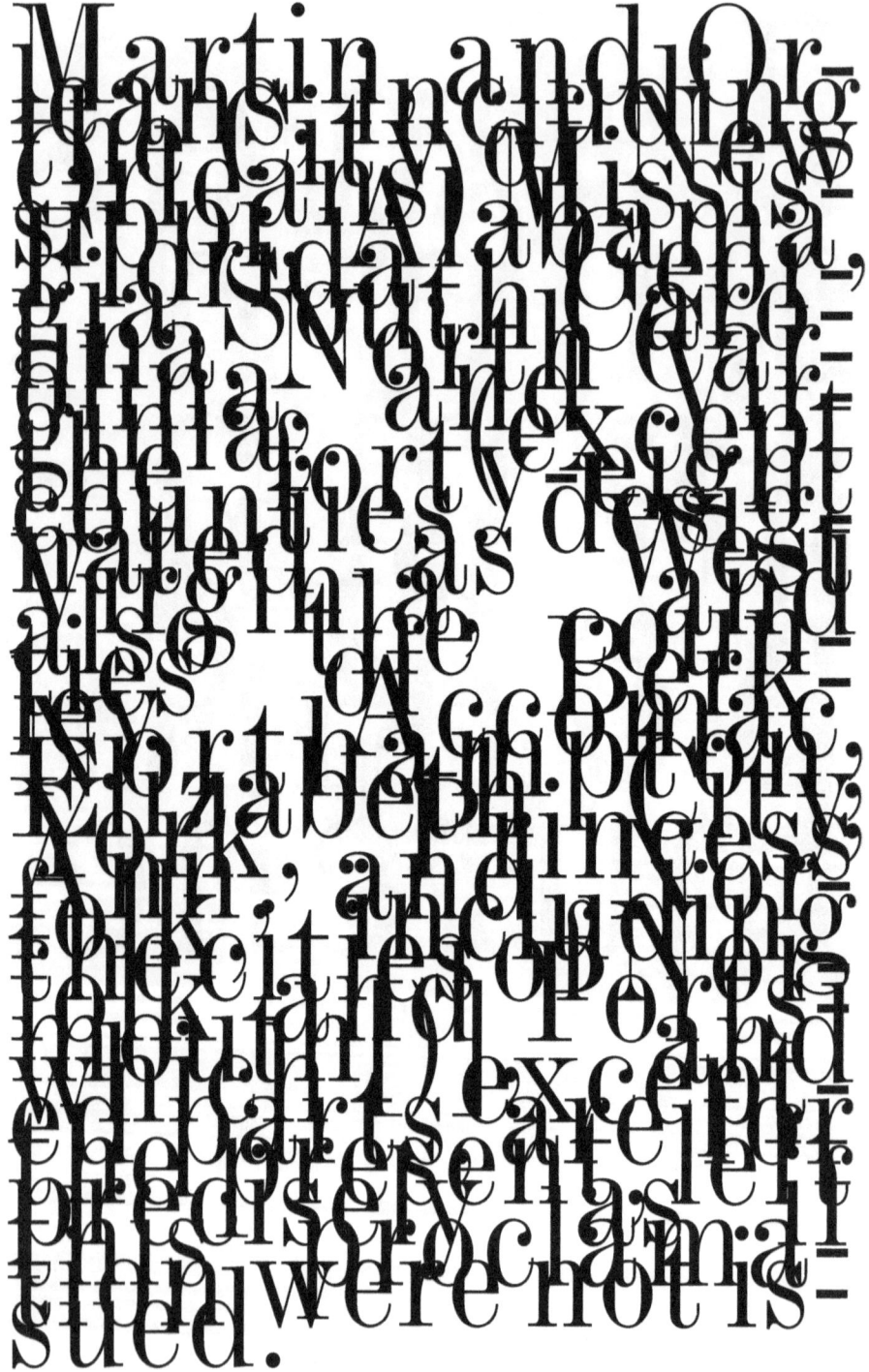

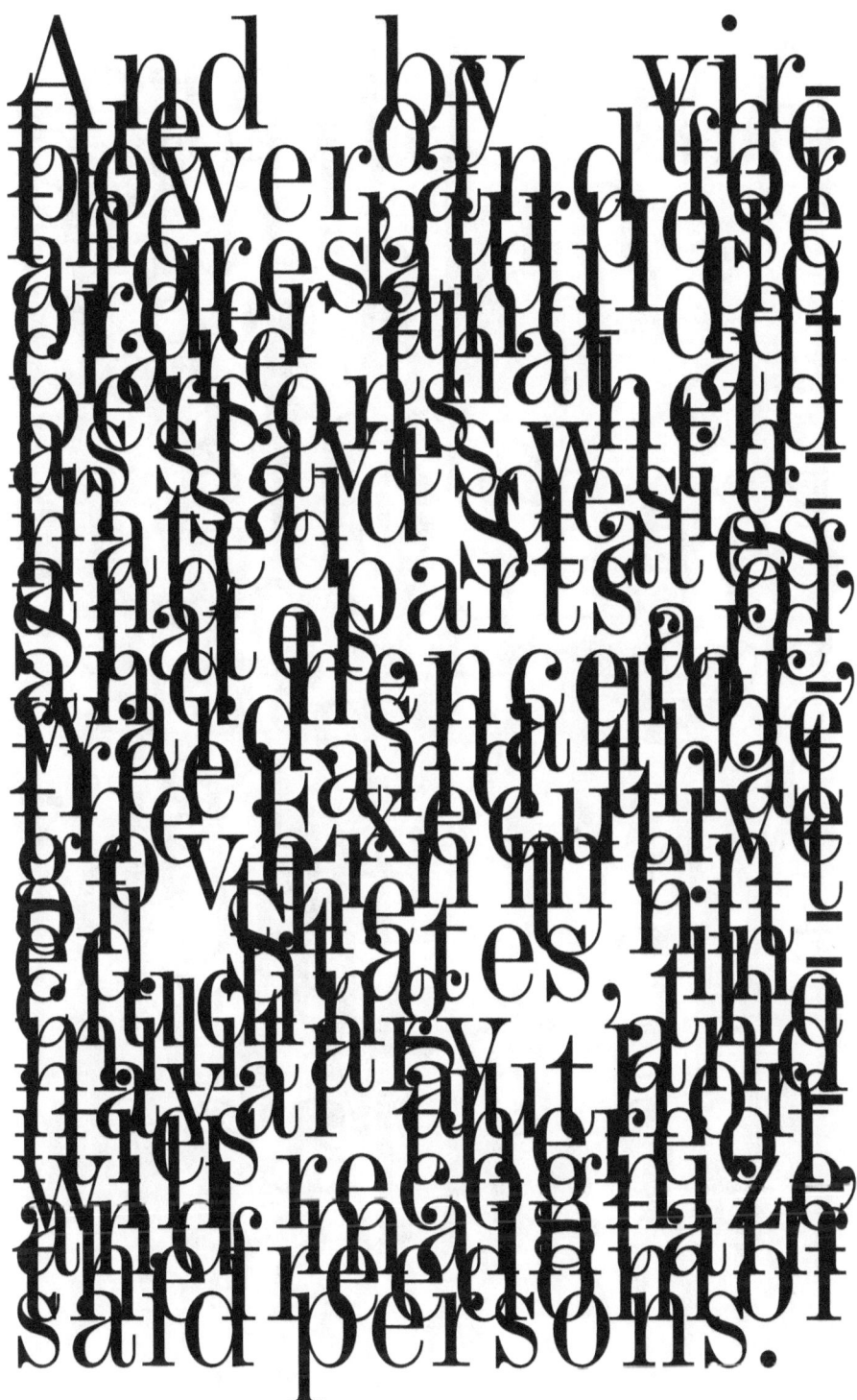

And by virtue of the power and for the purpose aforesaid, I do order and declare that all persons held as slaves within said designated States, and parts of States, are, and henceforward shall be free; and that the Executive government of the United States, including the military and naval authorities thereof, will recognize and maintain the freedom of said persons.

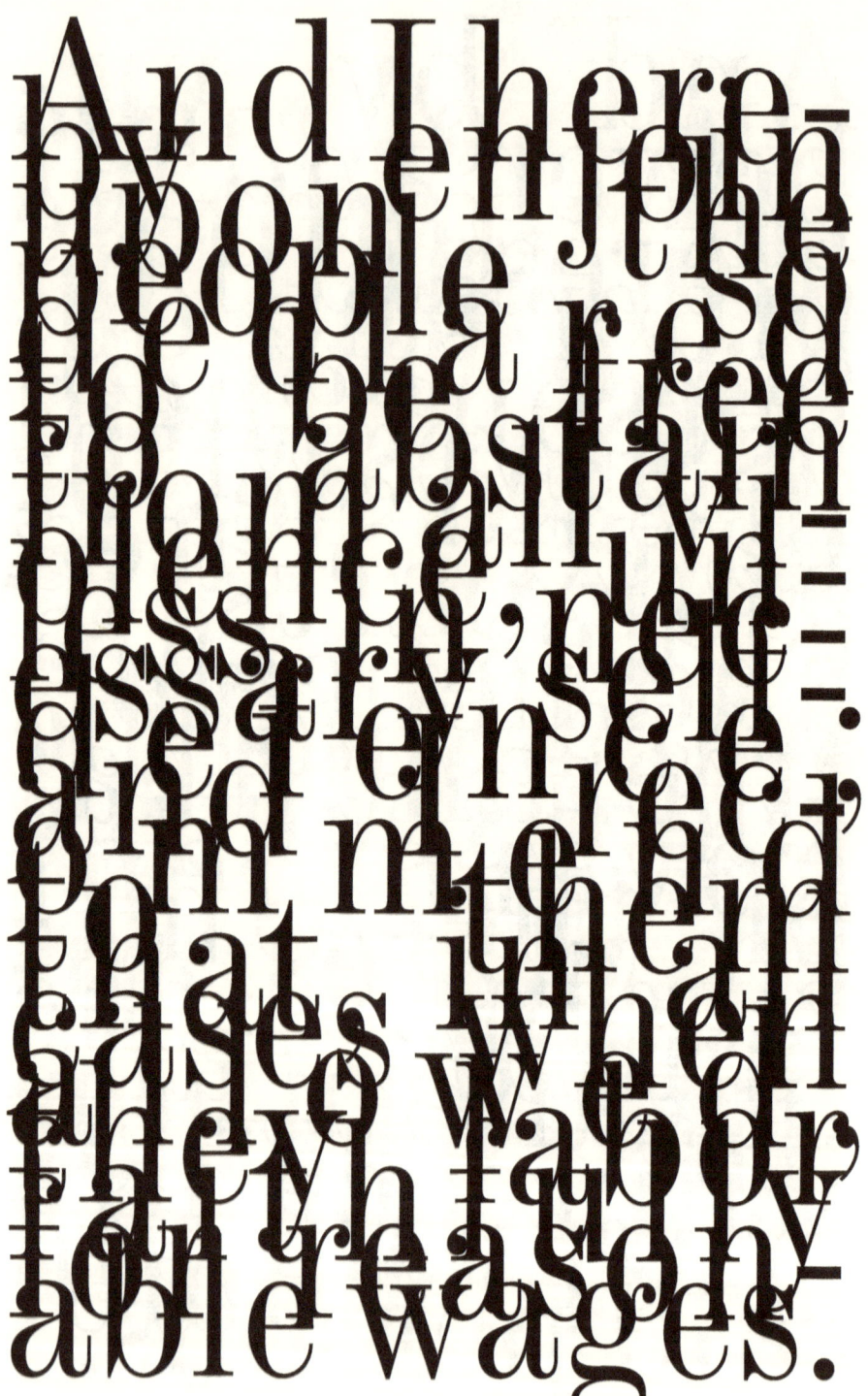

And I here-by enjoin the people to be free to abstain hence all unless in, necessary self-and m, te red that inc ases when allow ve or they vabor fairuly reason-able wages.

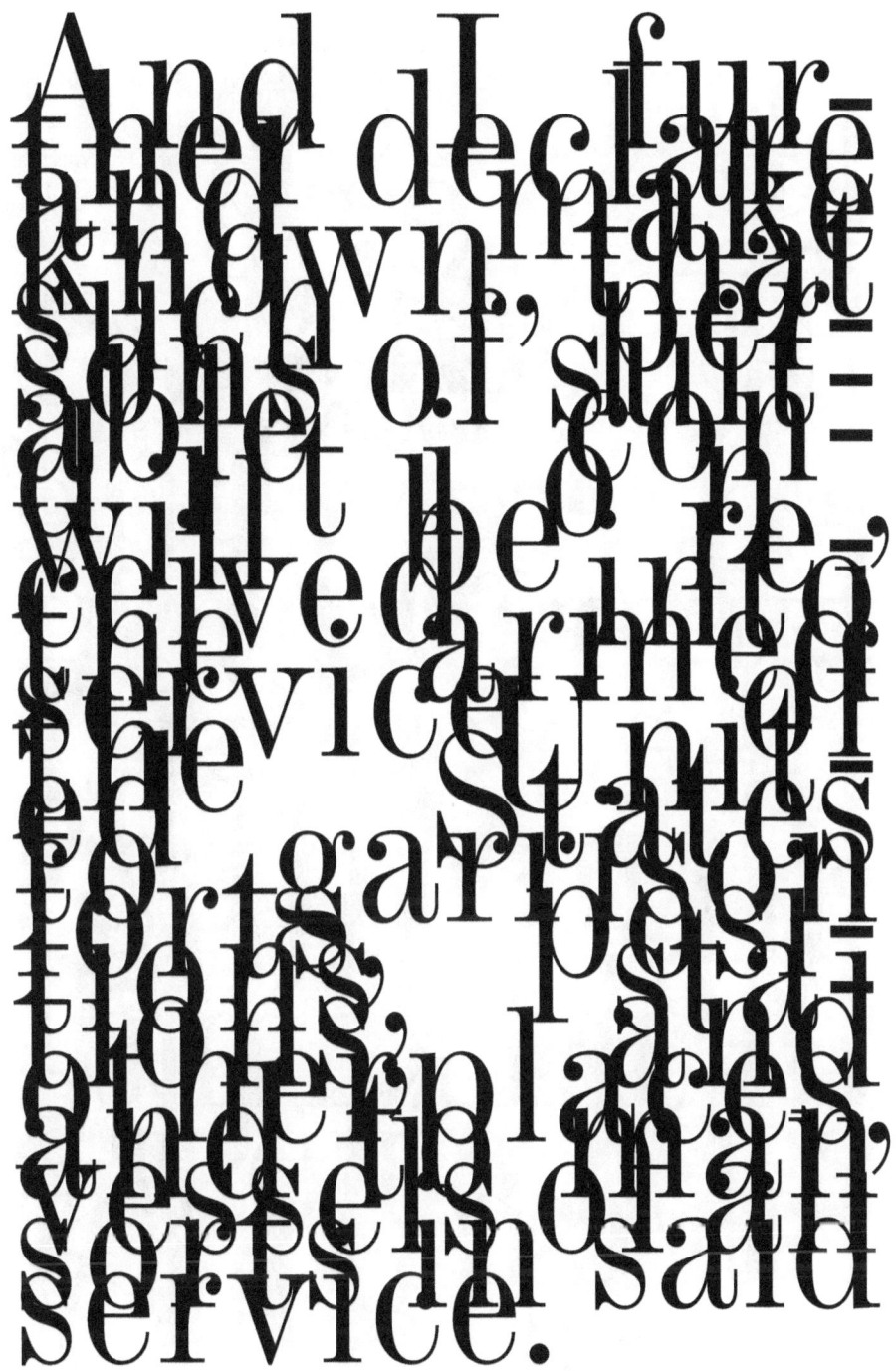

And I further declare and make known, that such persons will be received into the armed service of the United States at the garrisons, forts, positions, and other places, and vessels of all said service.

And upon this, we sincerely believed to be an act of warrant, by the transition to necessity invoked, the consideration of mankind and the gracious Almighty God.

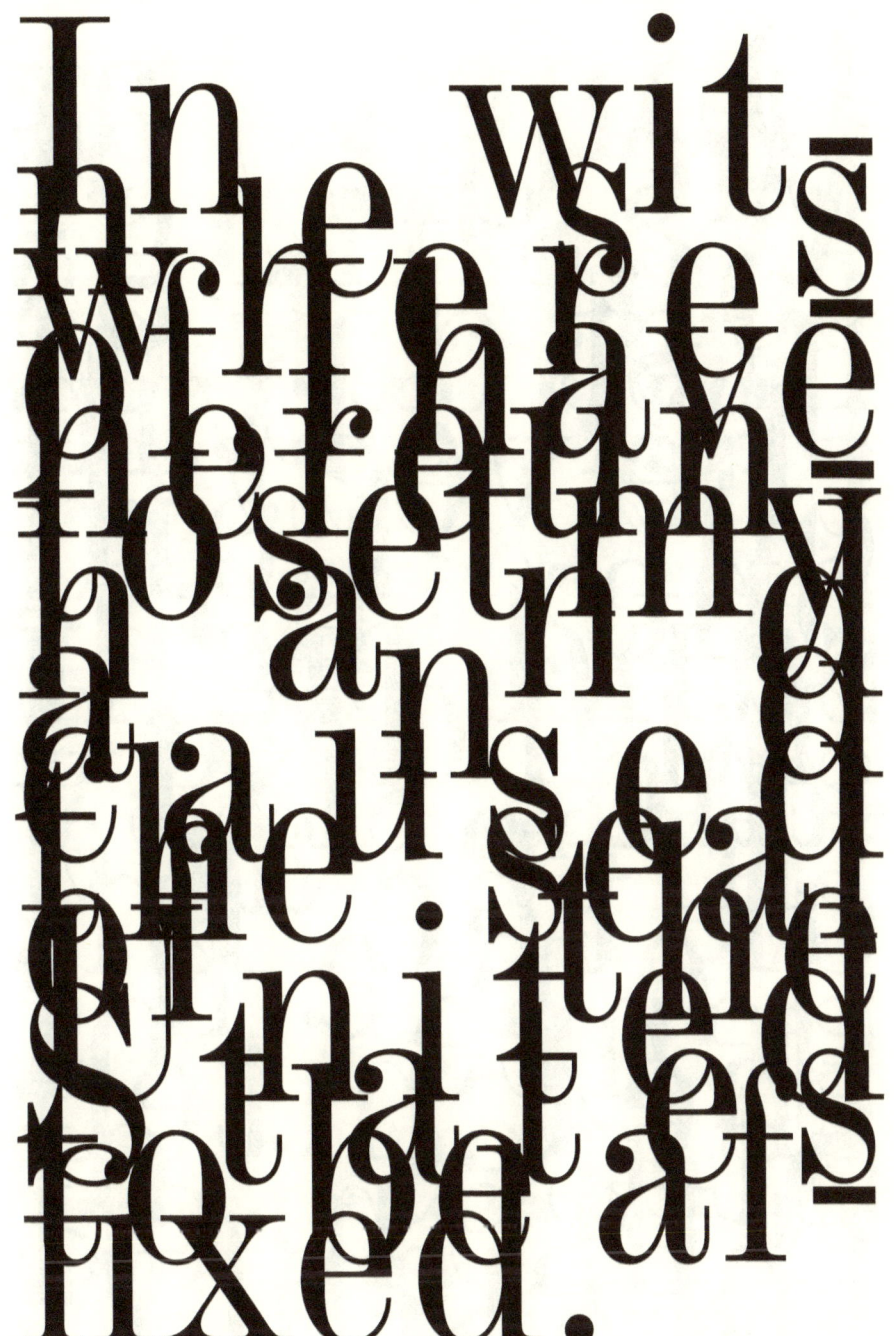

In witwherewherehaveoseetmythanausedthe seaunitedtatesbed afixed.

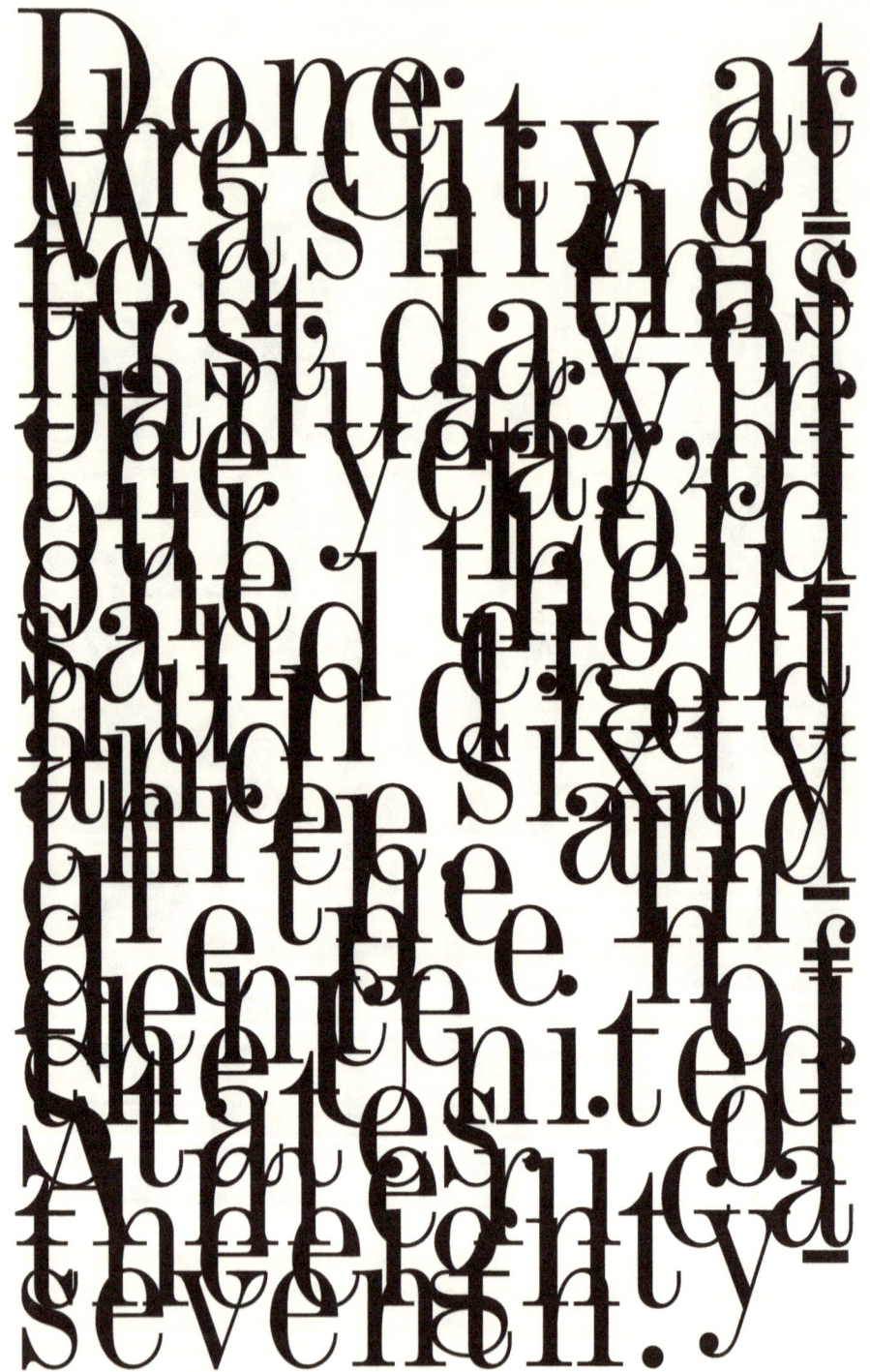

Done, at the city of Washington, this first day of January, in the year of our Lord one thousand eight hundred and sixty three, and of the Independence of the United States of America the eighty-seventh.

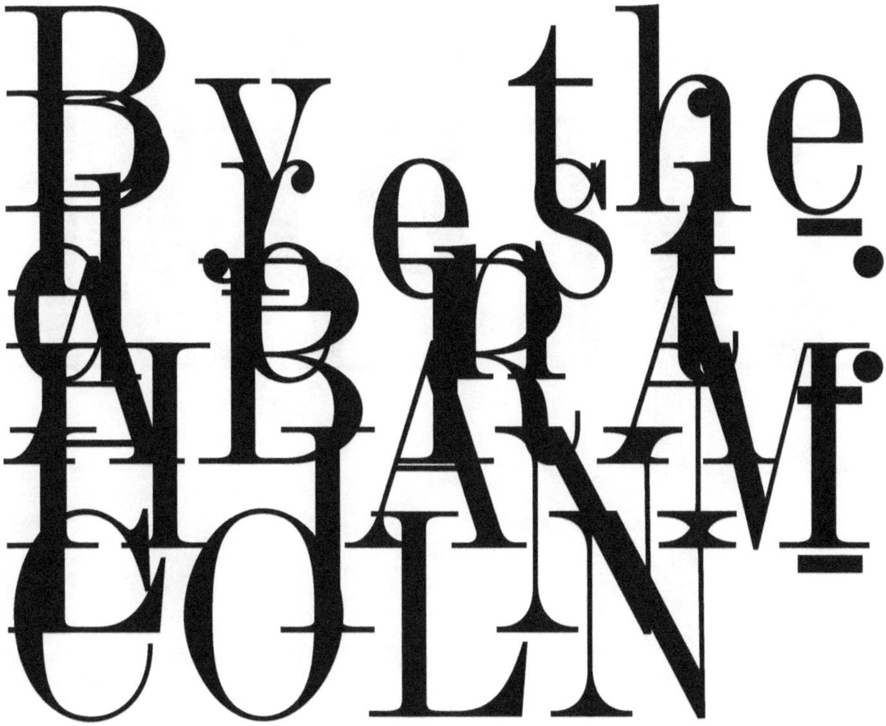

By the
President:
ABRAHAM
LINCOLN

WILLIAM H.

SEW-
ARD,
Sec-
reary
State.

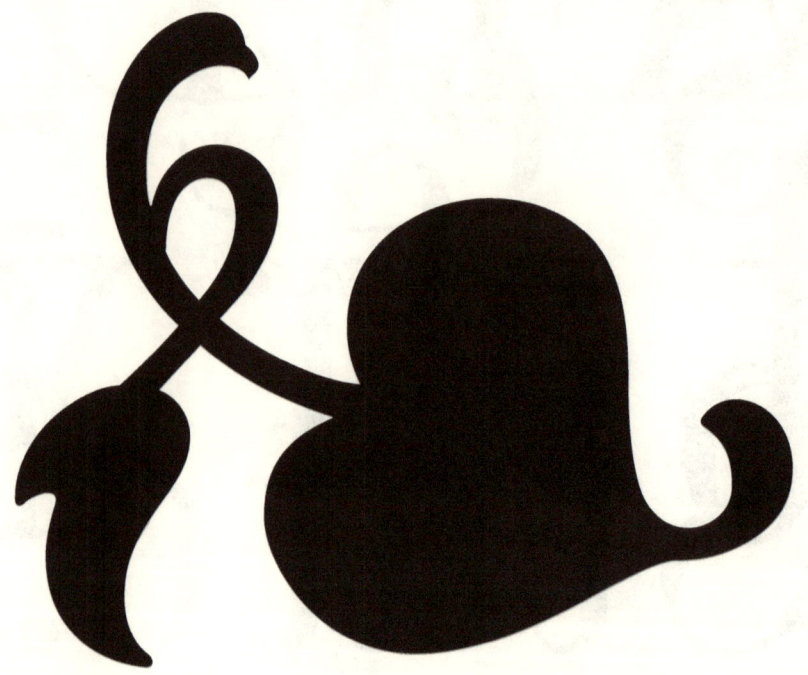

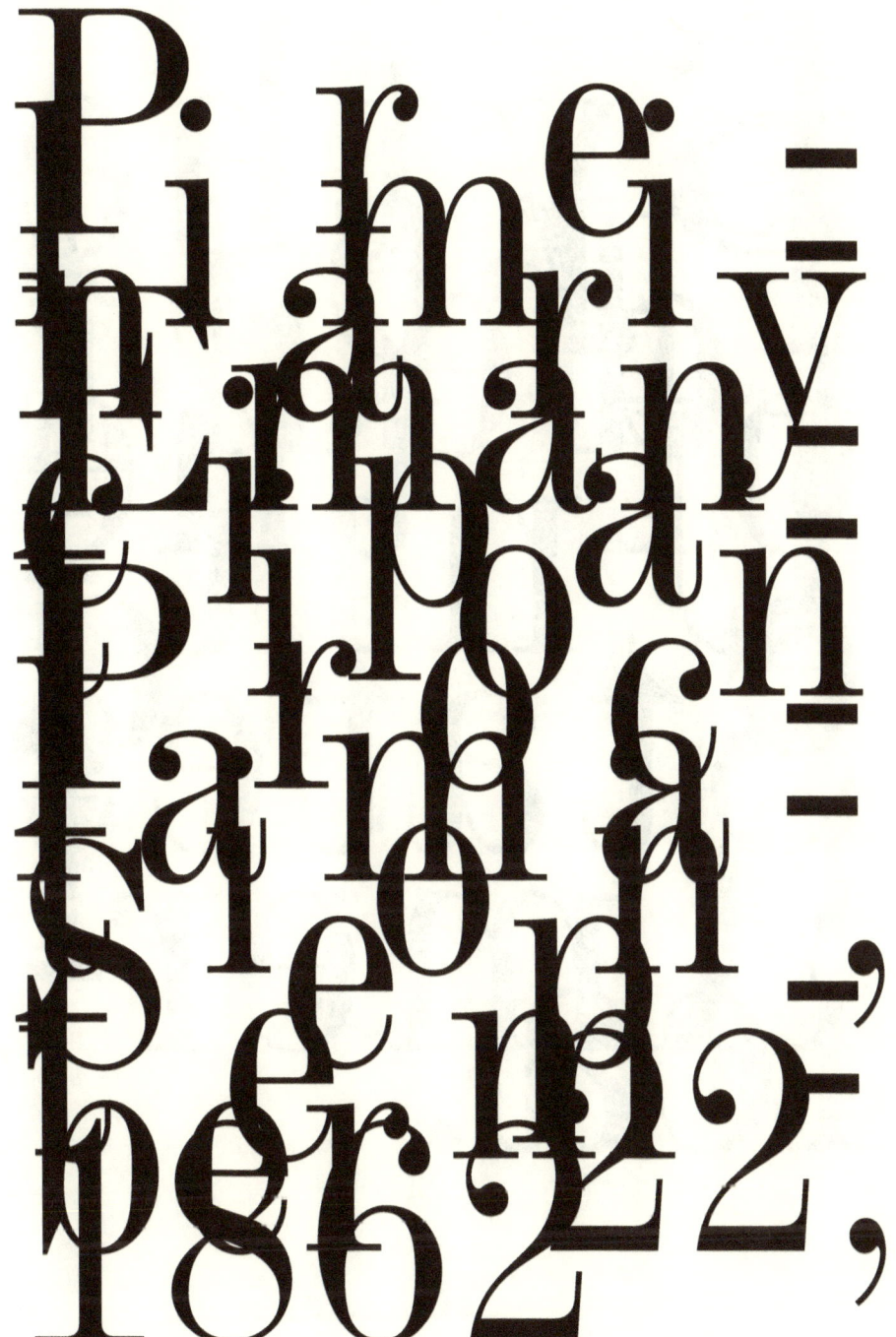

By the
President
of the
United
States
of America.

A Proclamation.

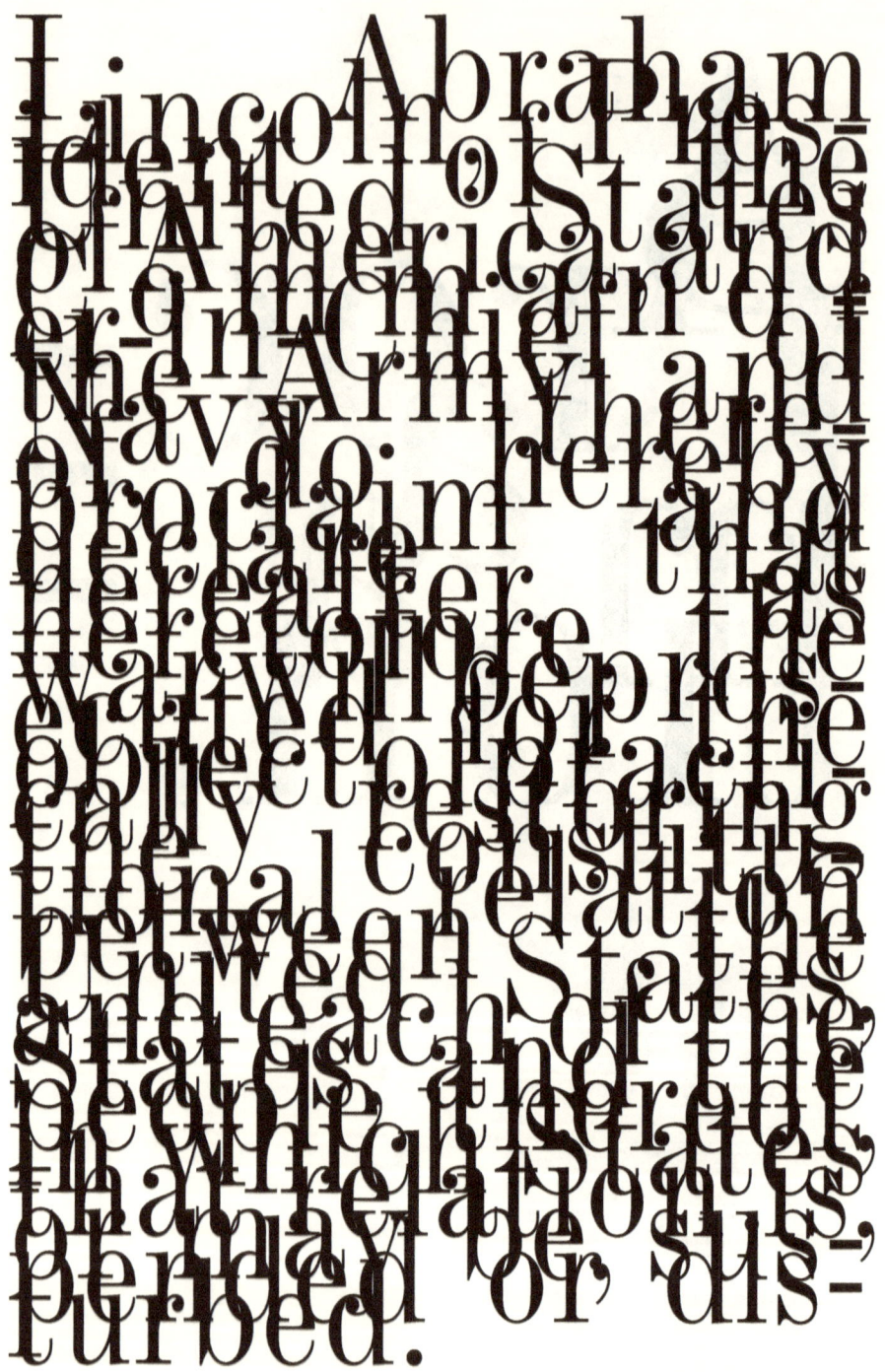

I, Abraham Lincoln, President of the United States of America, and Commander in Chief of the Army and Navy, do hereby proclaim and declare that hereafter, as heretofore, the war will be prosecuted for the object of practically restoring the constitutional relation between the United States and each of the States, and the people thereof, in which States that relation is, or may be, suspended or disturbed.

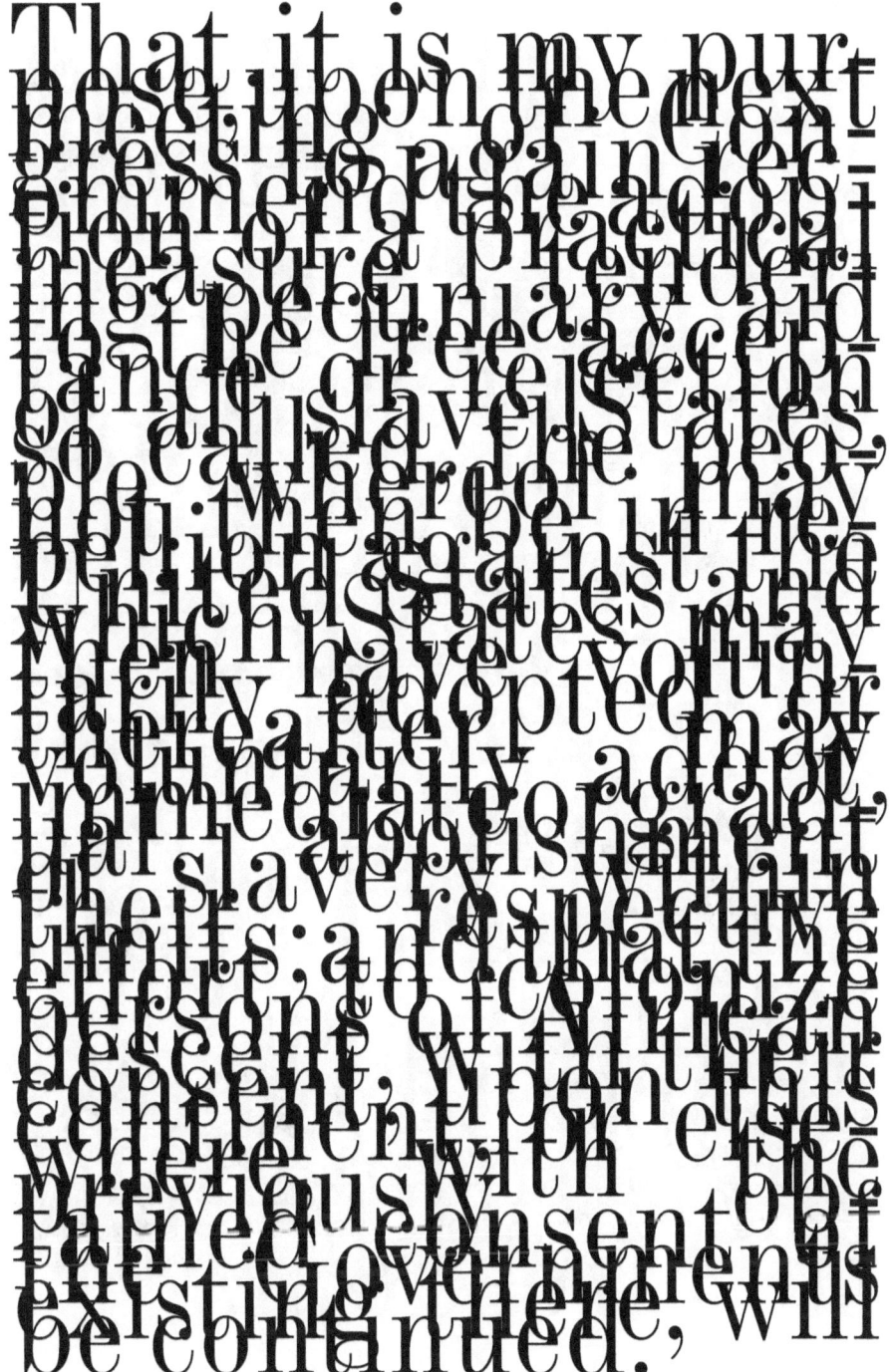

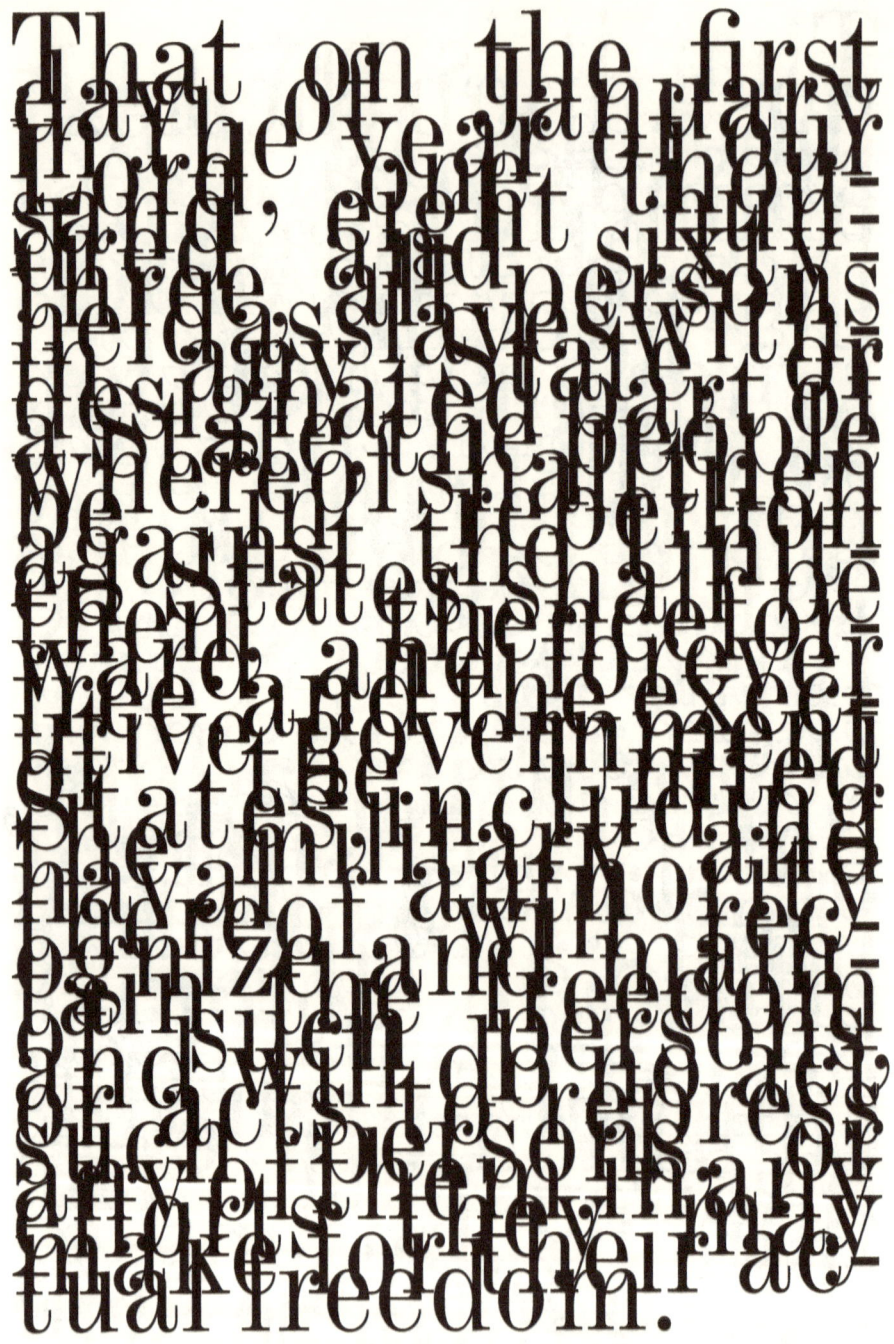

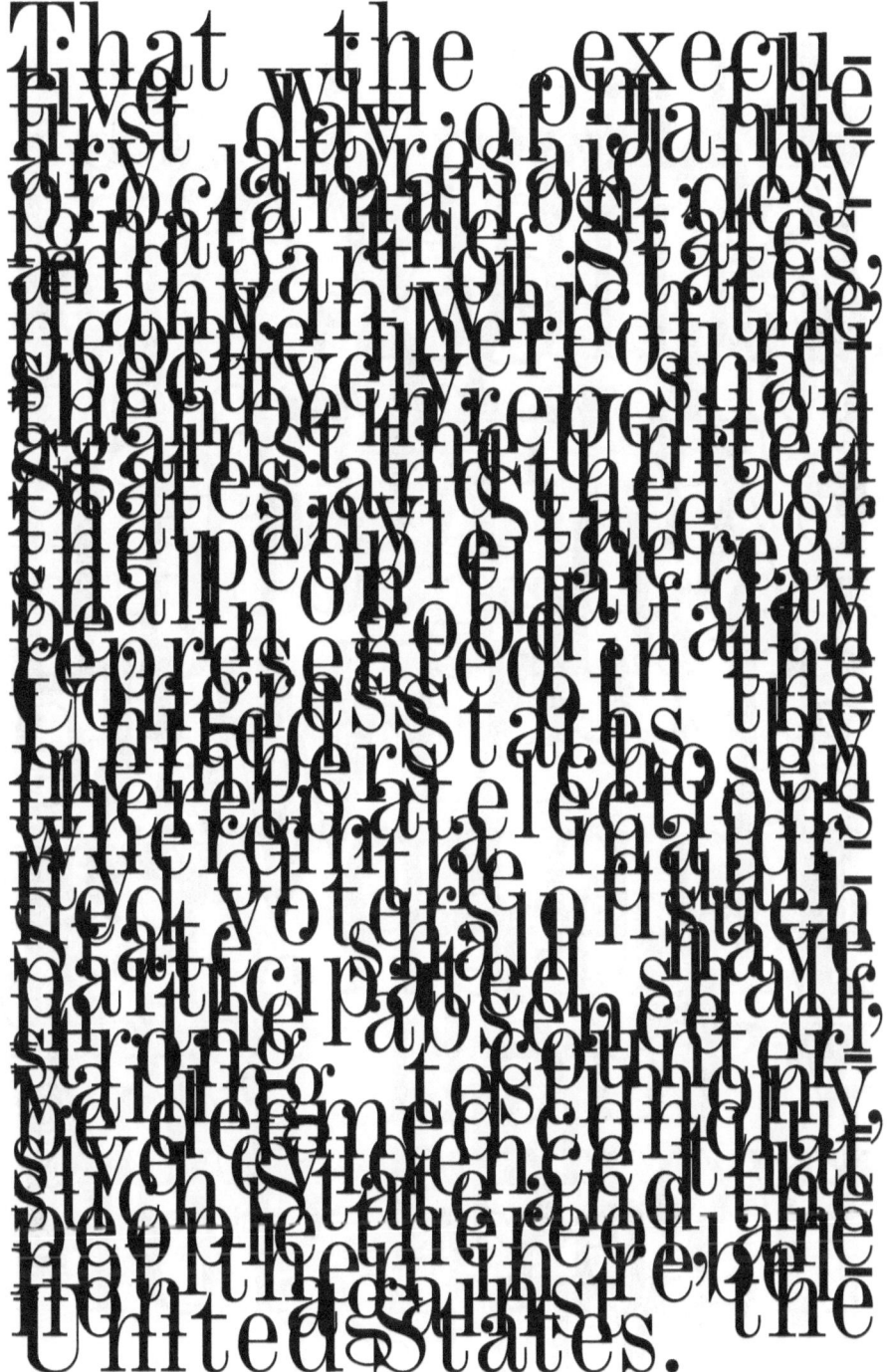

That the executive will, on the first day of January aforesaid, by proclamation, designate the States and parts of States, if any, in which the people thereof respectively shall then be in rebellion against the United States; and the fact that any State, or the people thereof, shall on that day be, in good faith, represented in the Congress of the United States by members chosen thereto at elections wherein a majority of the qualified voters of such State shall have participated, shall, in the absence of strong countervailing testimony, be deemed conclusive evidence that such State, and the people thereof, have not then been in rebellion against the United States.

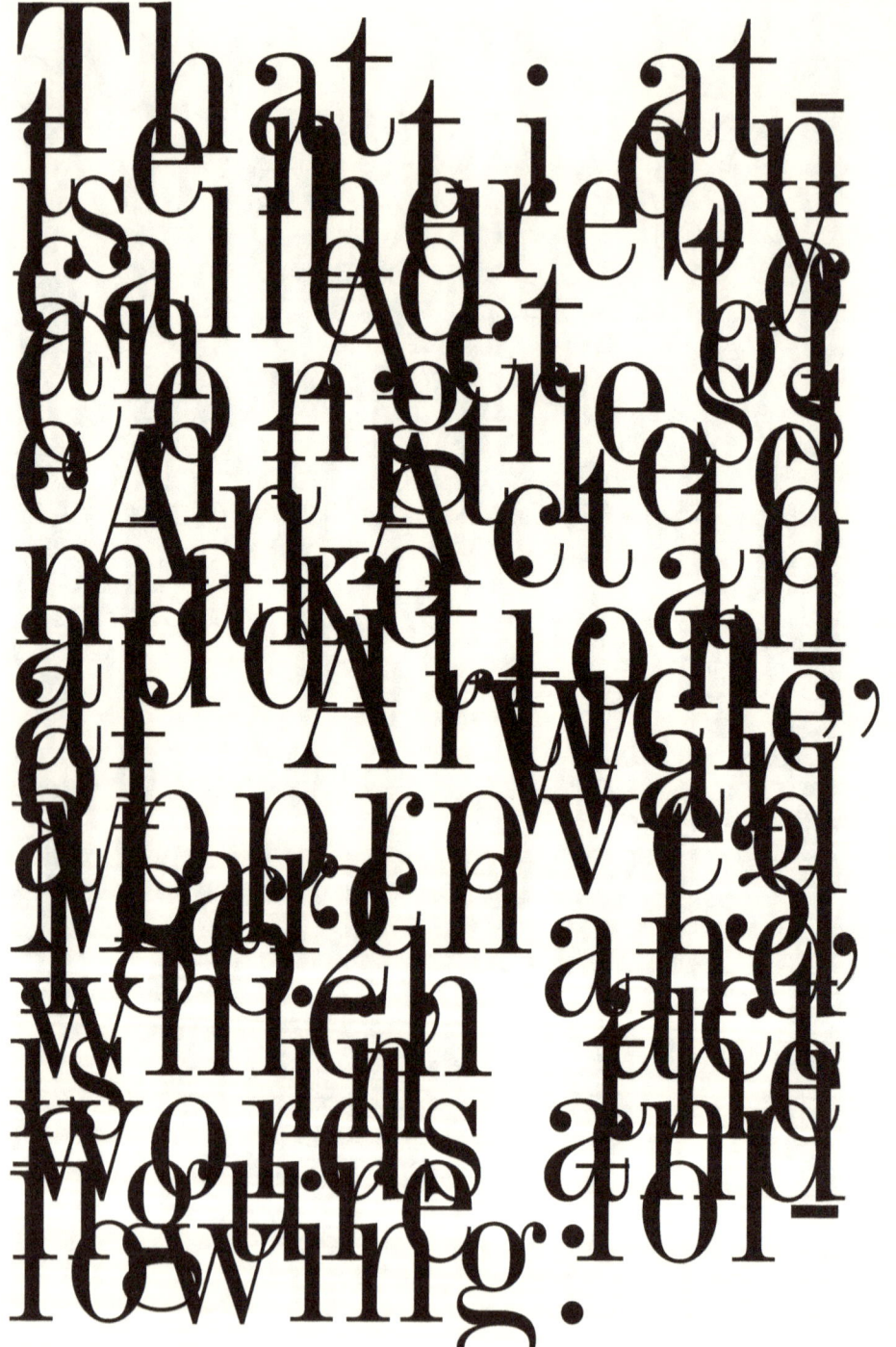

That i attension hereby called it that Act of Congress an Act entitled make an action At were, Approved March, which and, words and the following:

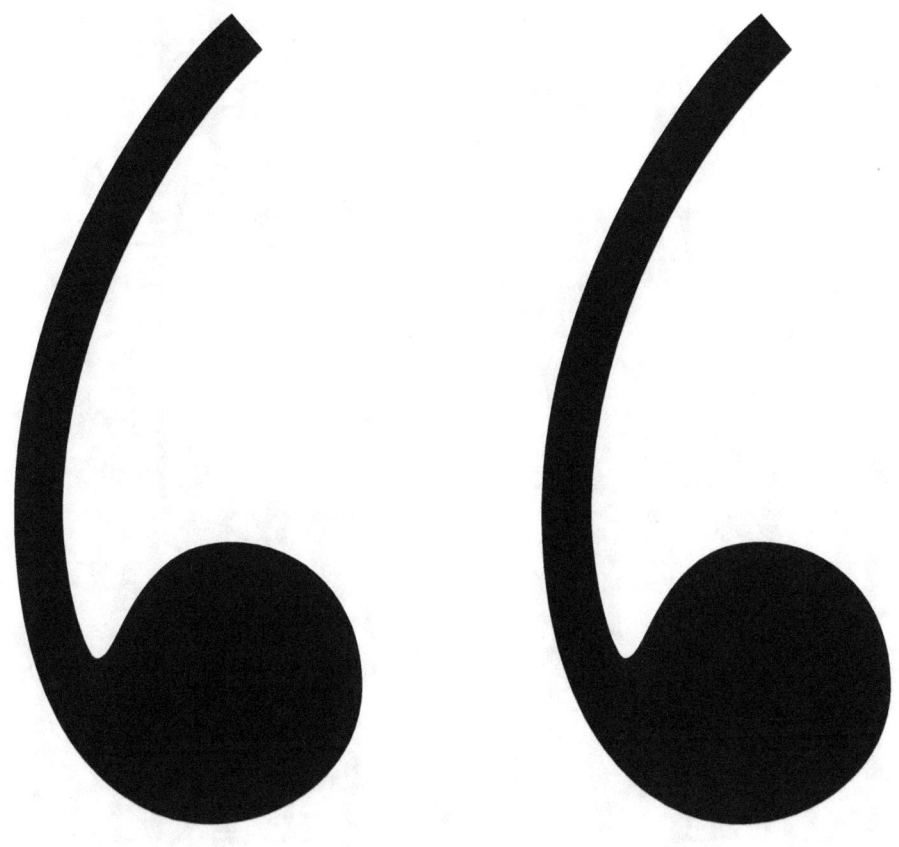

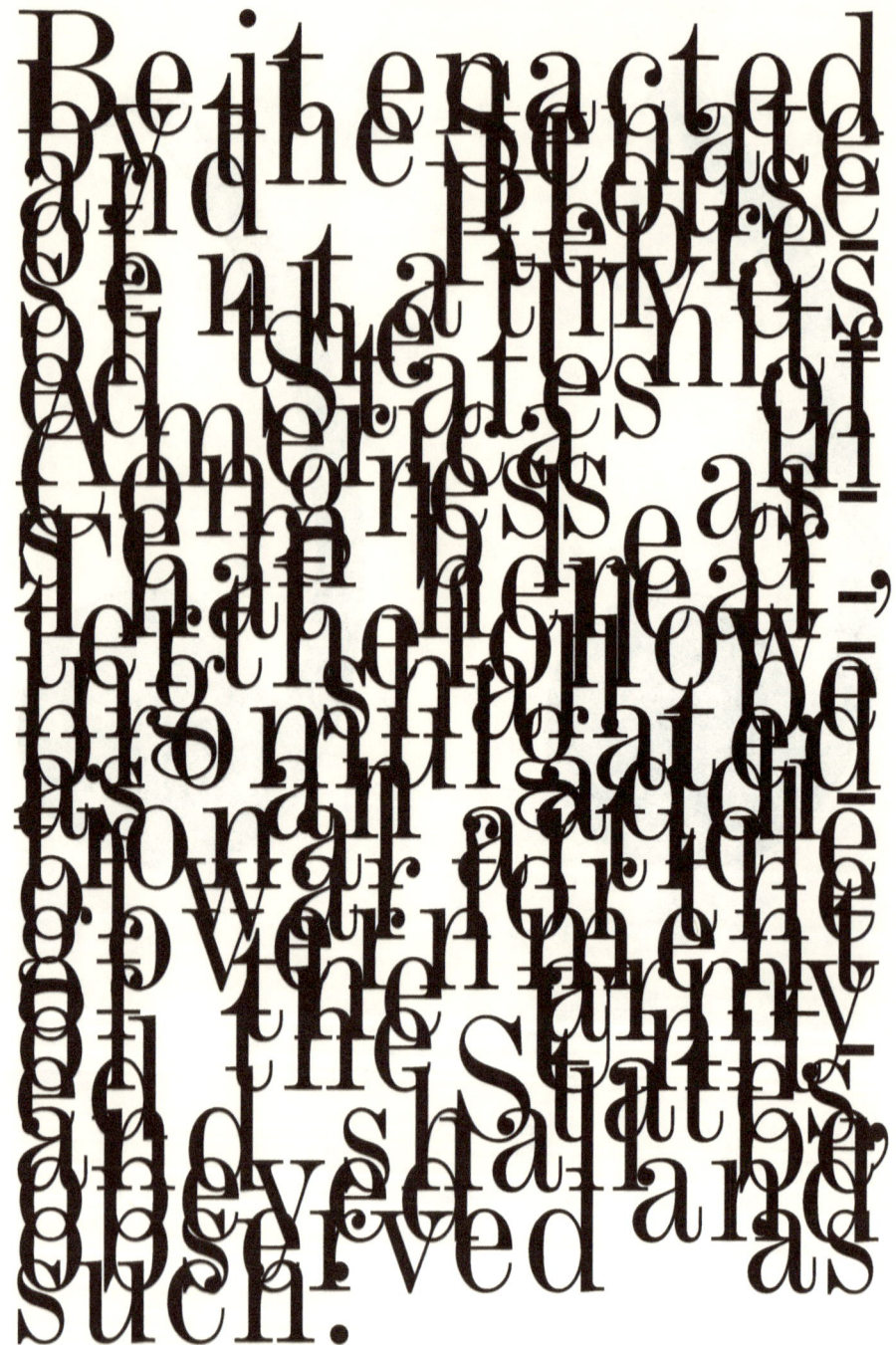

Be it enacted by the Senate and House of Representatives of the United States of America in Congress assembled, that hereafter the following promulgated additional article of government for the army of the South and shall be observed and as such.

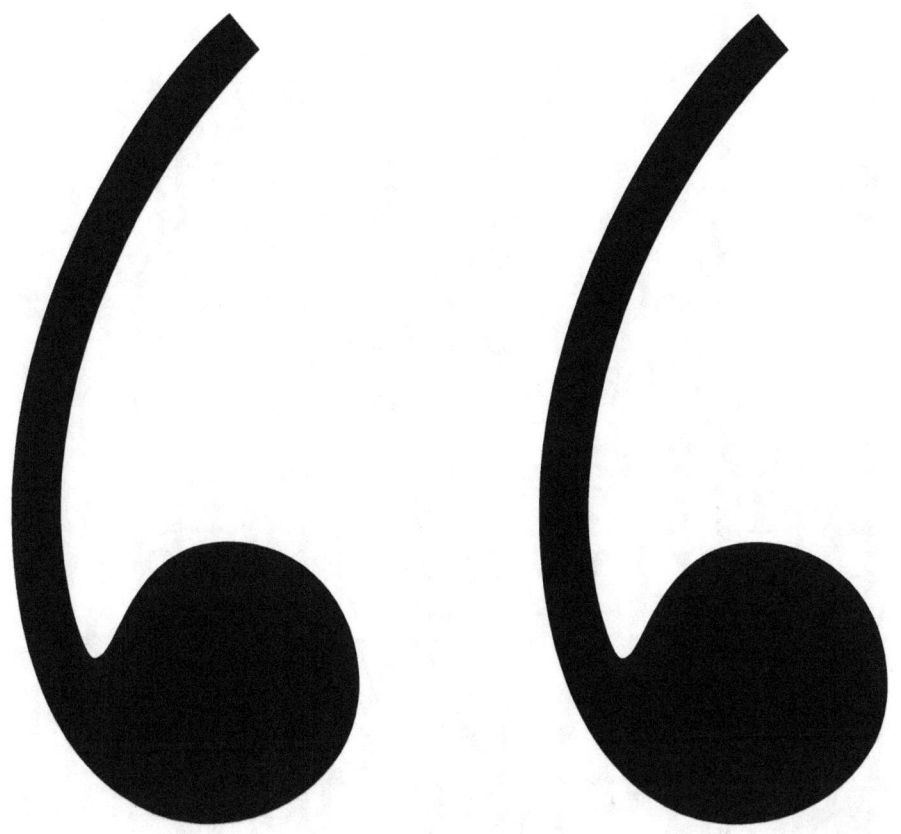

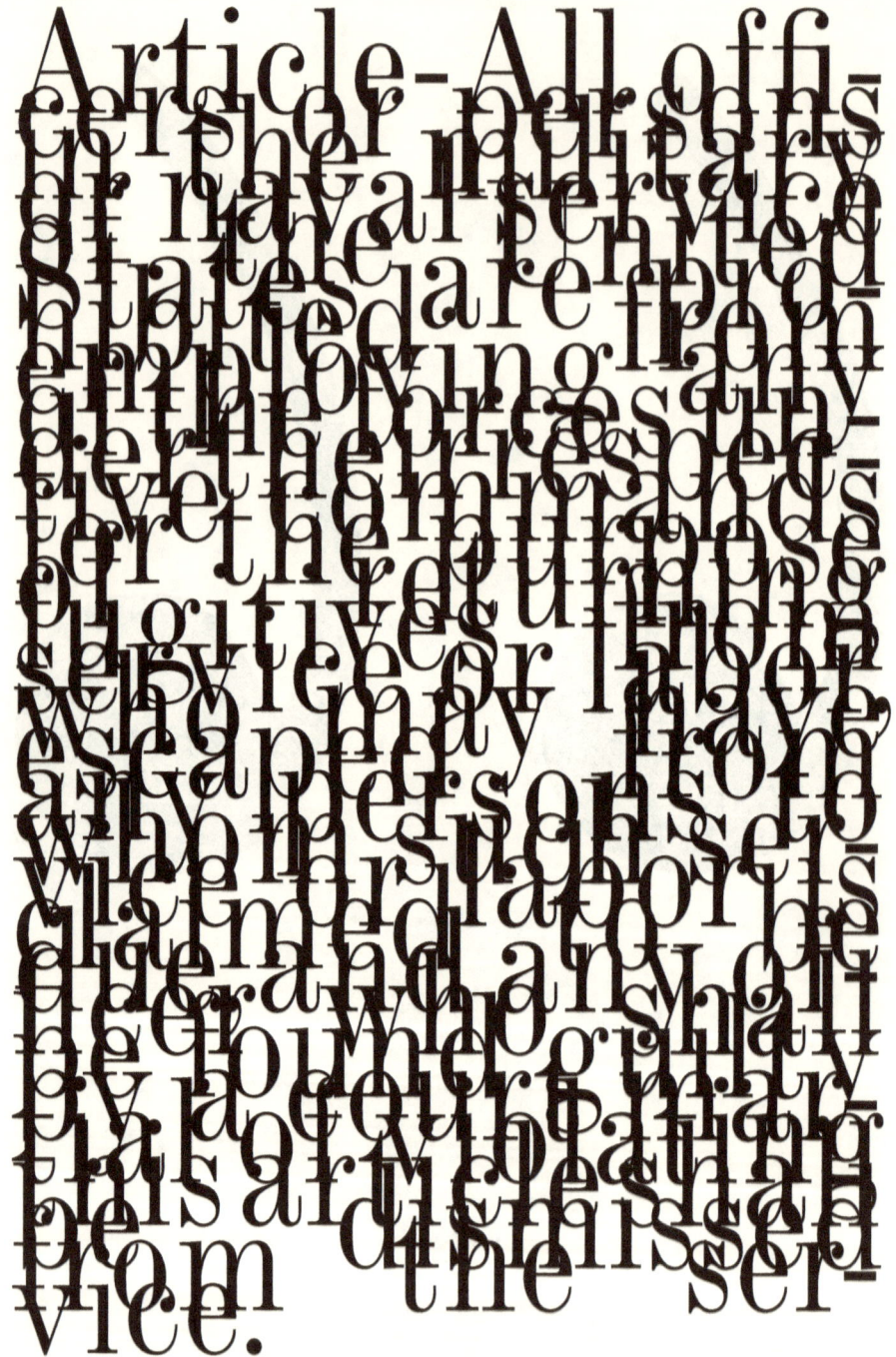

Article-All offi-cers, or other persons of the naval service of the United States, are prohibited from employing any of the forces under their respective commands for the purpose of returning fugitives from service or labor who may have escaped from any persons to whom such service or labor is claimed to be due, and any officer who shall be found guilty of violating this article shall be dismissed from the service.

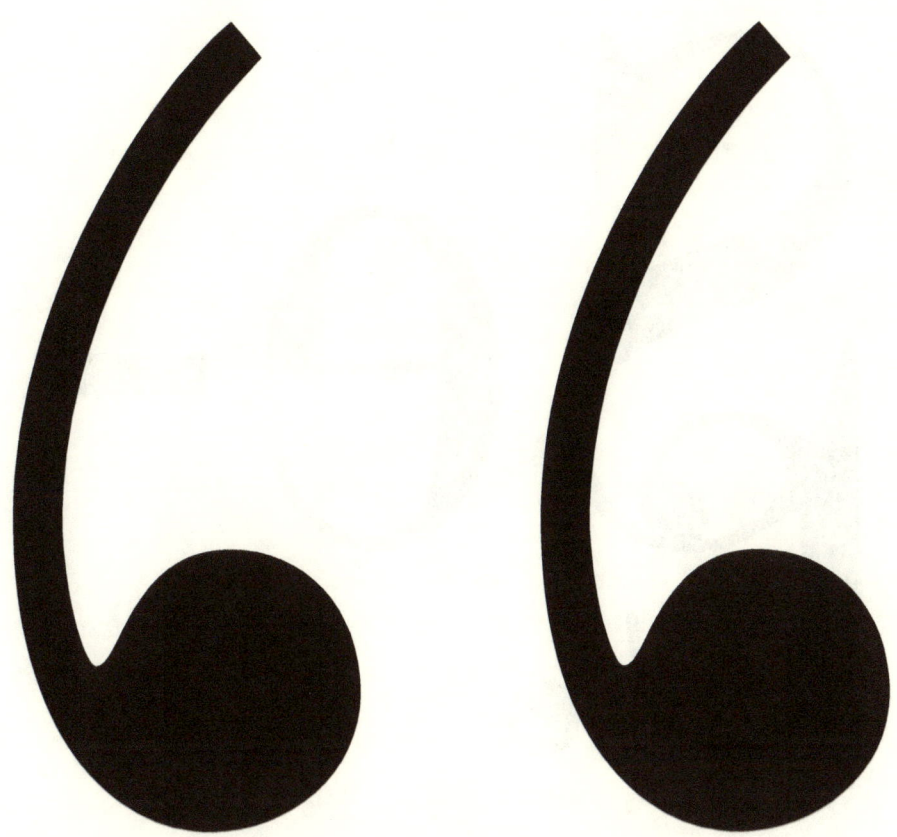

Se-

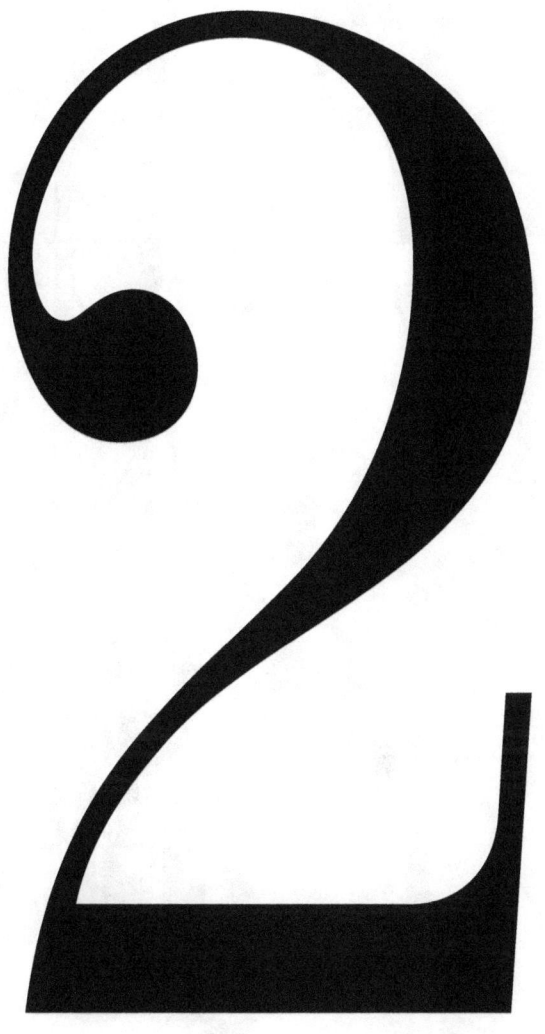

And further, at
this act,
make room and its
page.

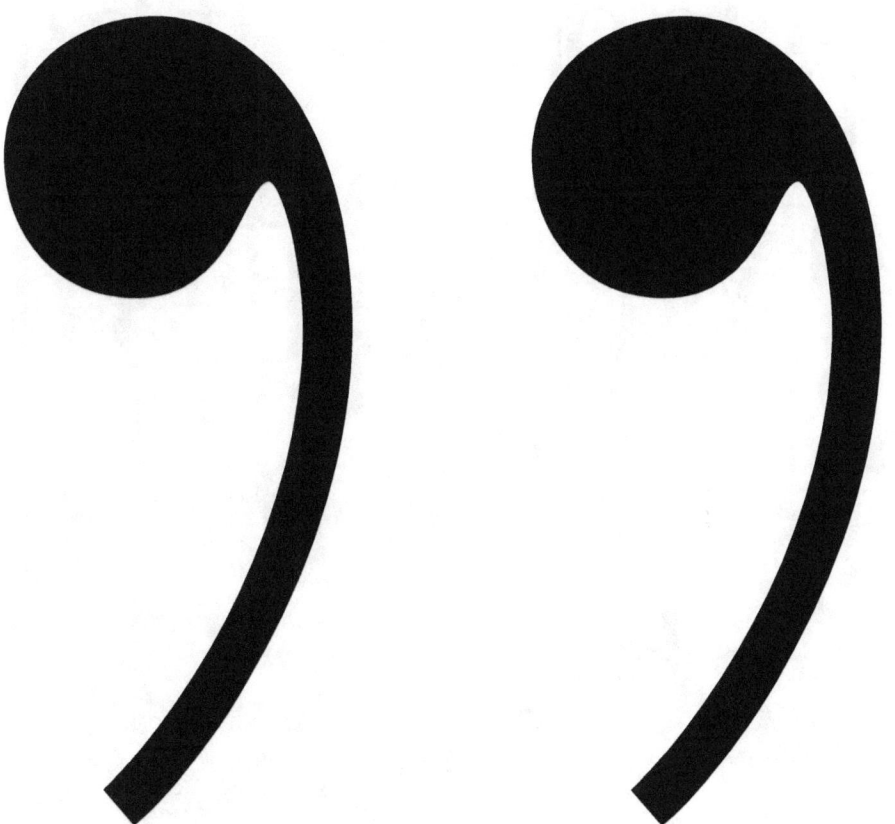

Also to the ninth and tenth sections of an Act entitled "An Act to suppress insurrection, to punish treason and rebellion, to seize and confiscate property of rebels, and for other purposes," approved July 17, 1864, which are the words and figures following:

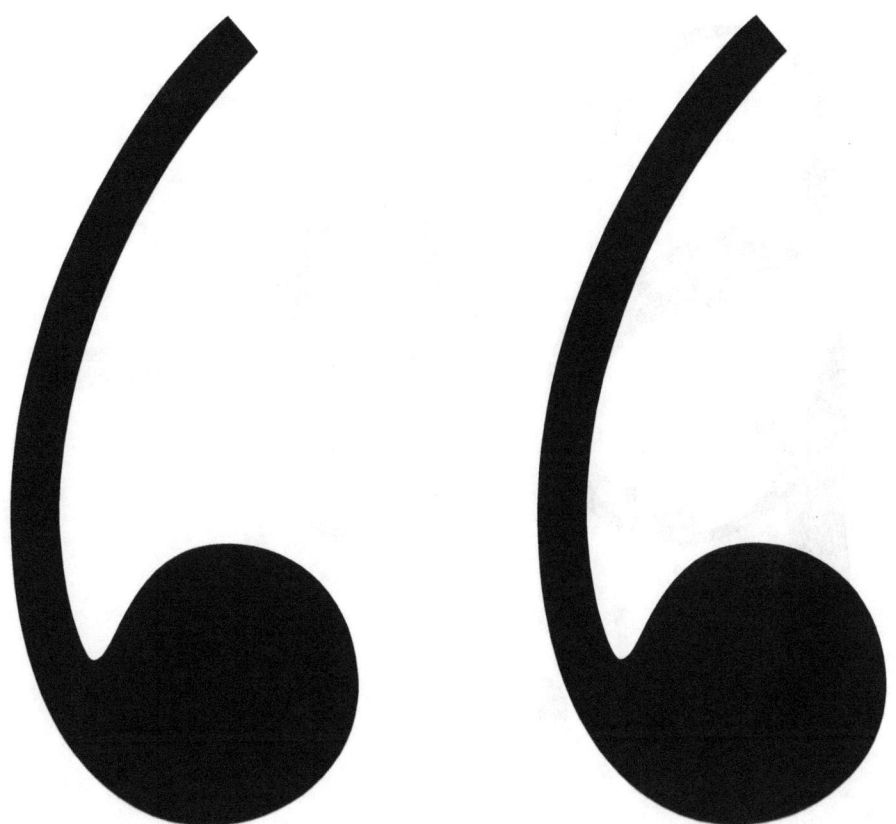

Se-
c.

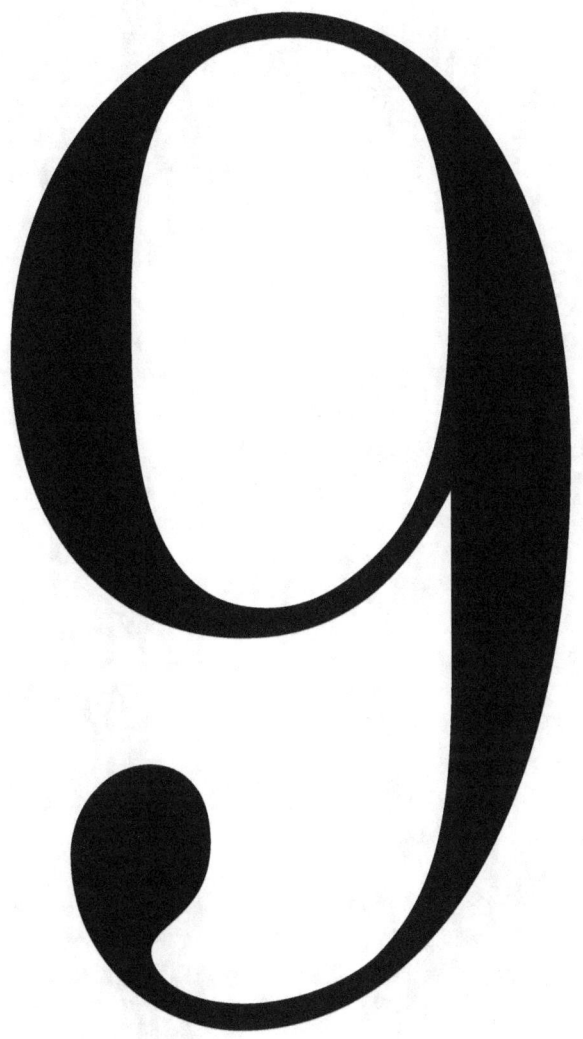

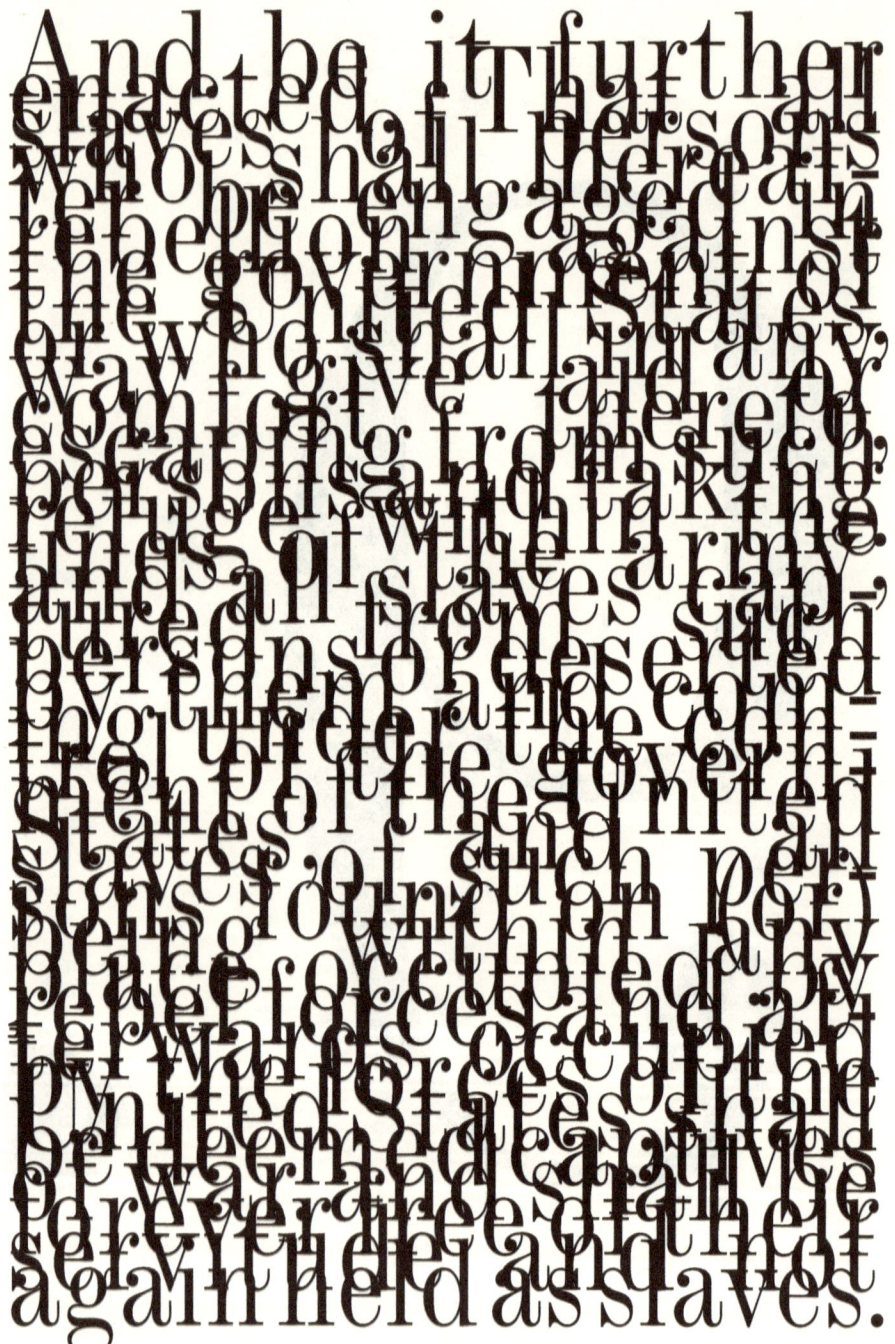

And be it further enacted, That all persons who shall have been engaged against the government of the United States, or who shall in any way give aid or comfort thereto, escaping from such persons and taking refuge within the lines of the army; and all slaves captured from such persons or deserted by them and coming under the control of the government of the United States; and all slaves of such persons found on, being within, any place occupied by rebel forces and afterwards occupied by the forces of the United States, shall be deemed captives of war, and shall be forever free of their servitude, and not again held as slaves.

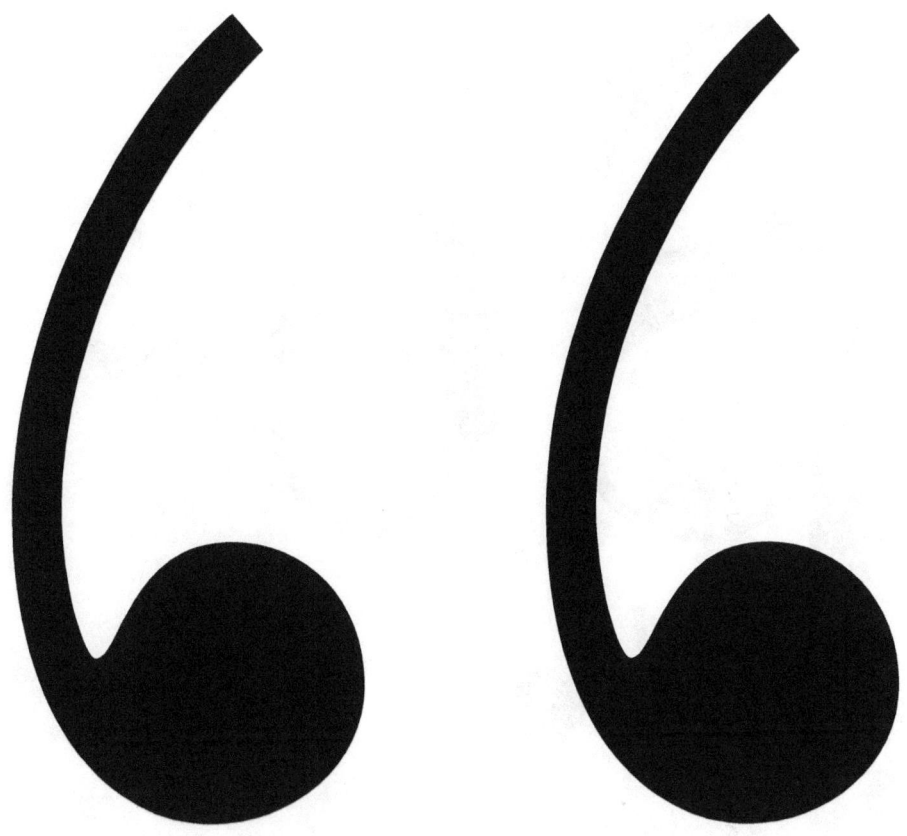

Se-
pec.

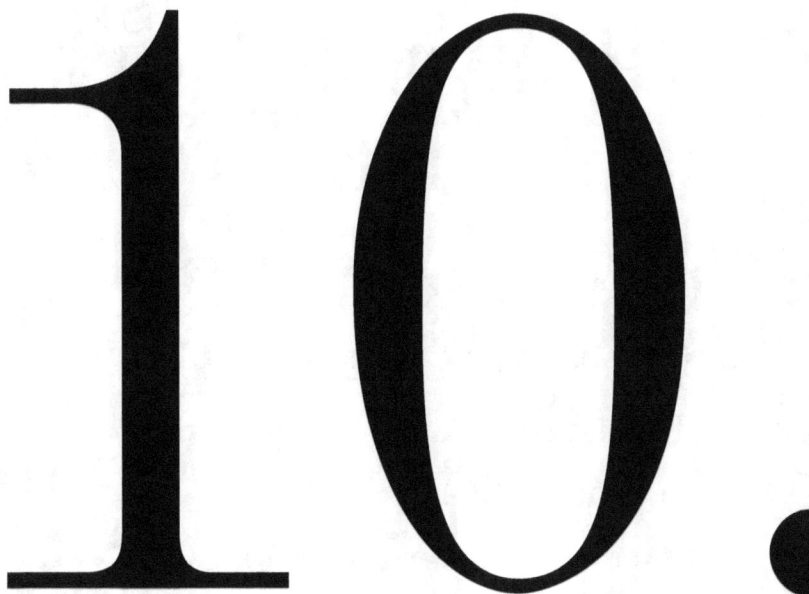

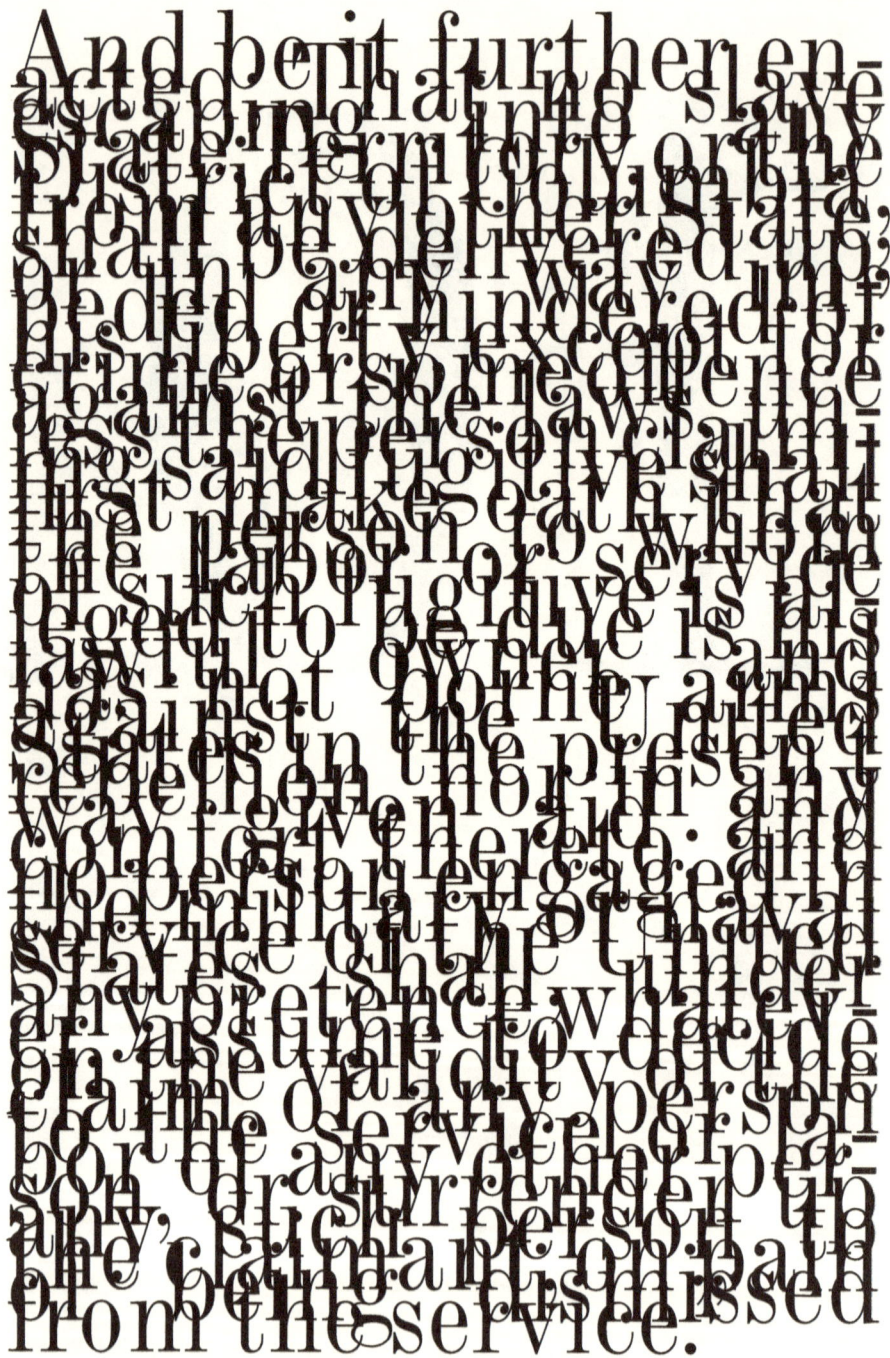

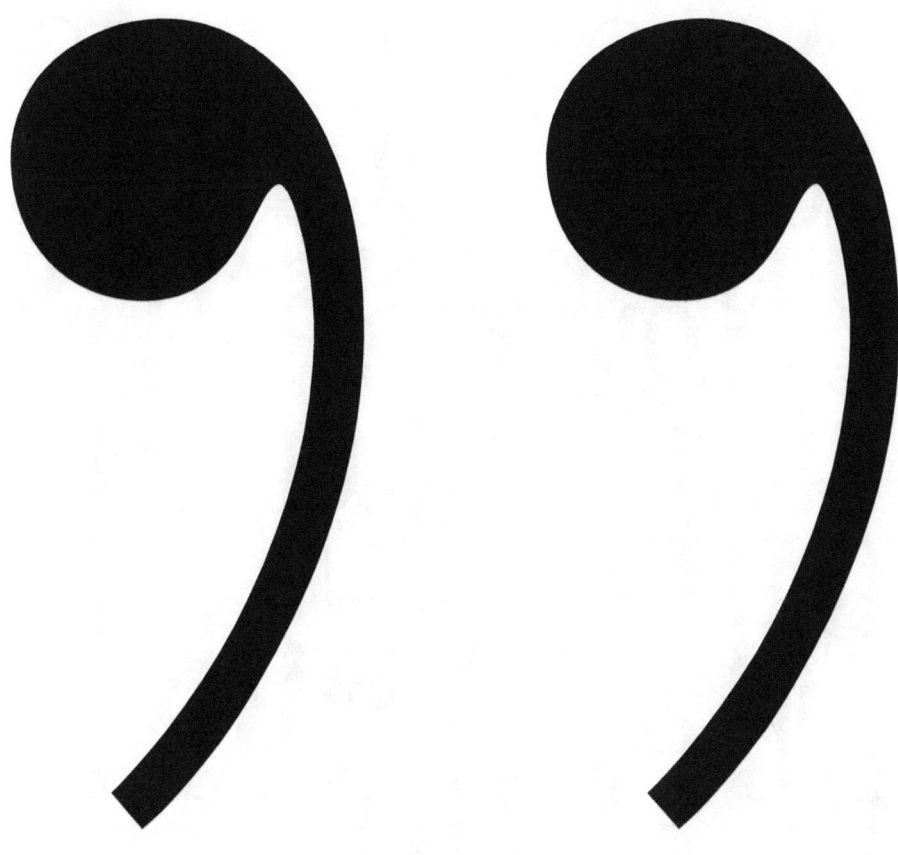

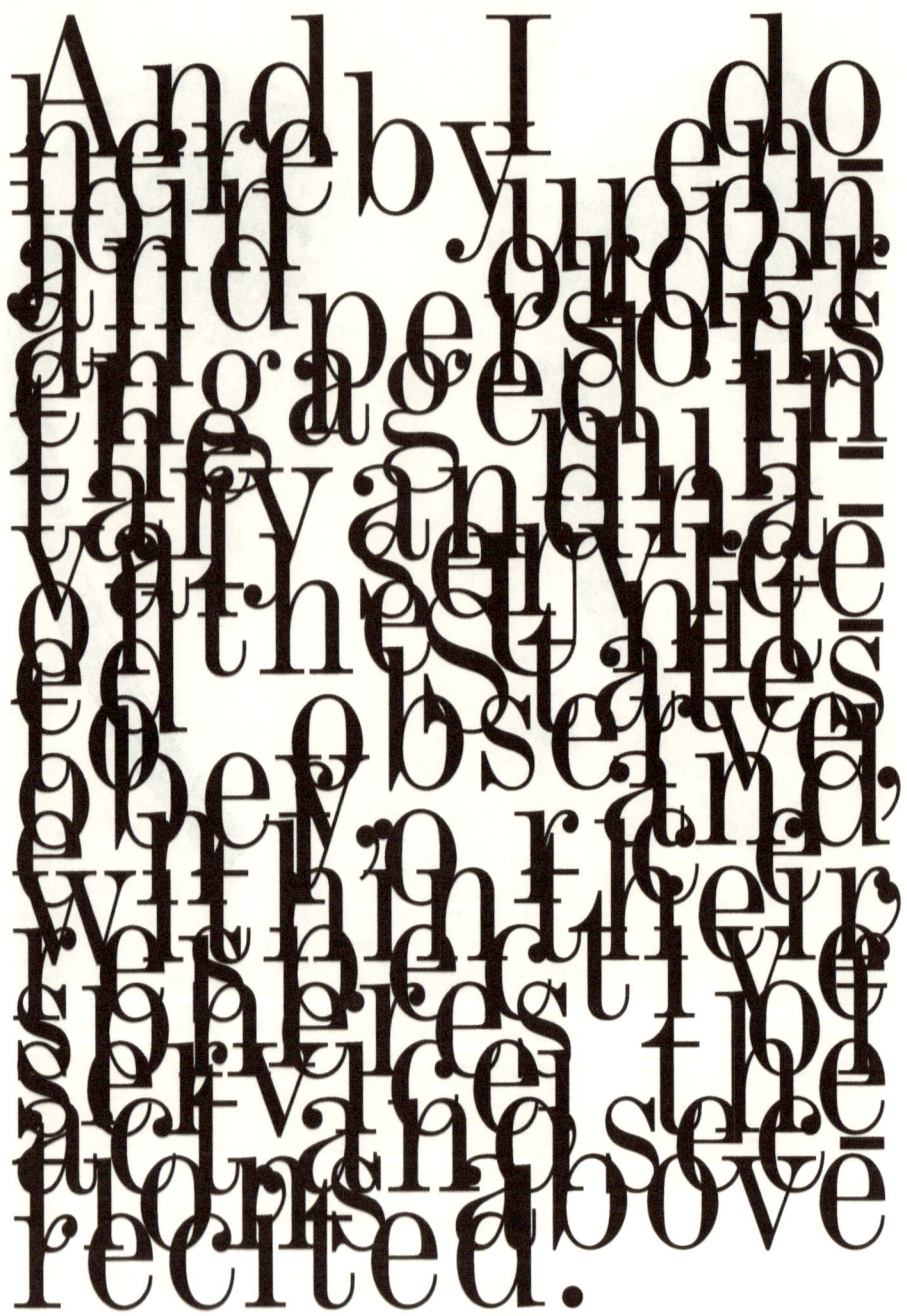

And I do hereby enjoin and order all persons engaged in the military and naval service of the United States to observe and obey, within their respective spheres of service, the acts and sections above recited.

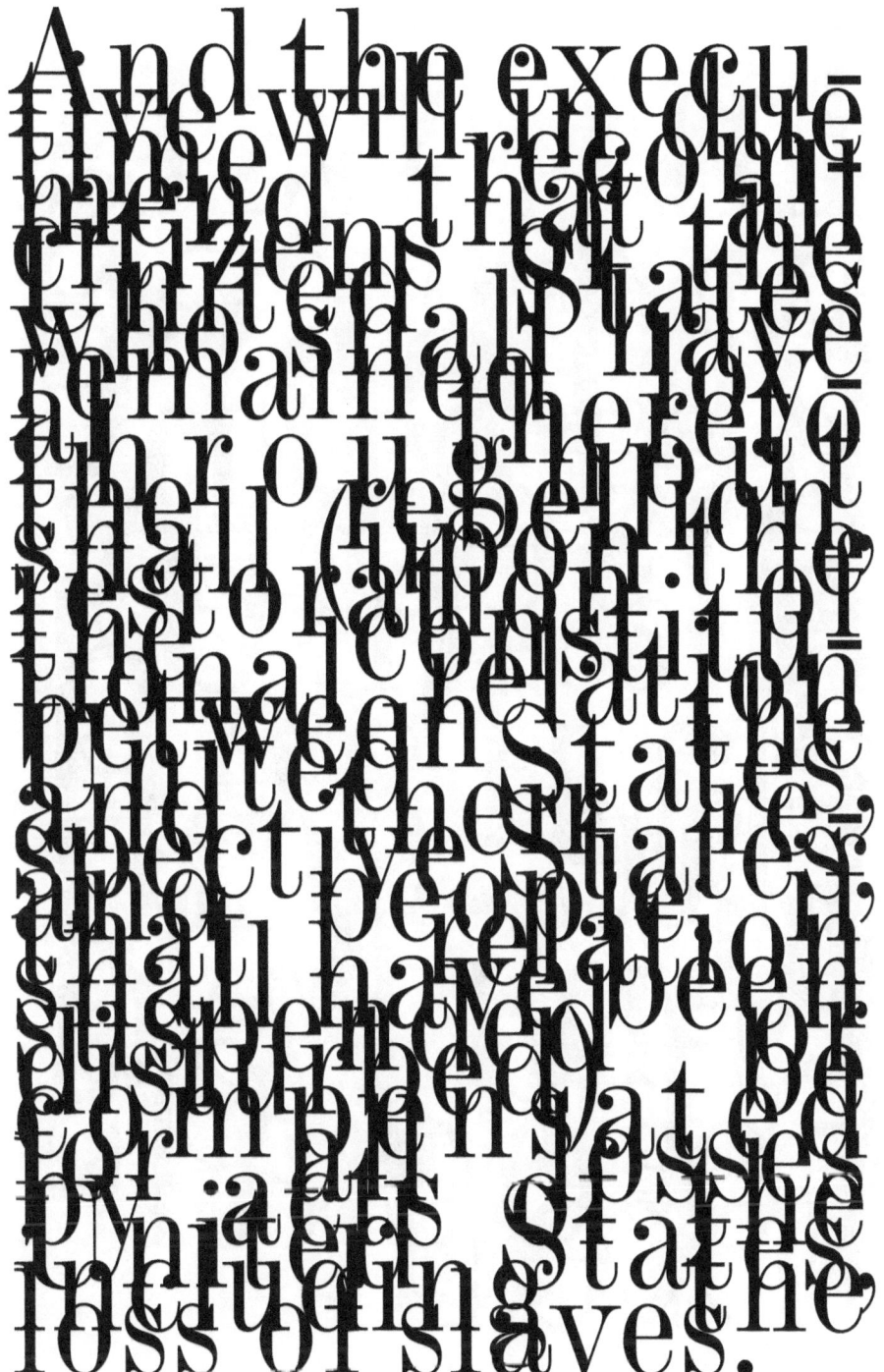

And the executive will recommend that all citizens of the United States who shall have remained loyal thereto throughout the rebellion shall (upon the restoration of the constitutional relation between the United States and their respective States and people, if that relation shall have been suspended or disturbed) be compensated for all losses by acts of the United States including the loss of slaves.

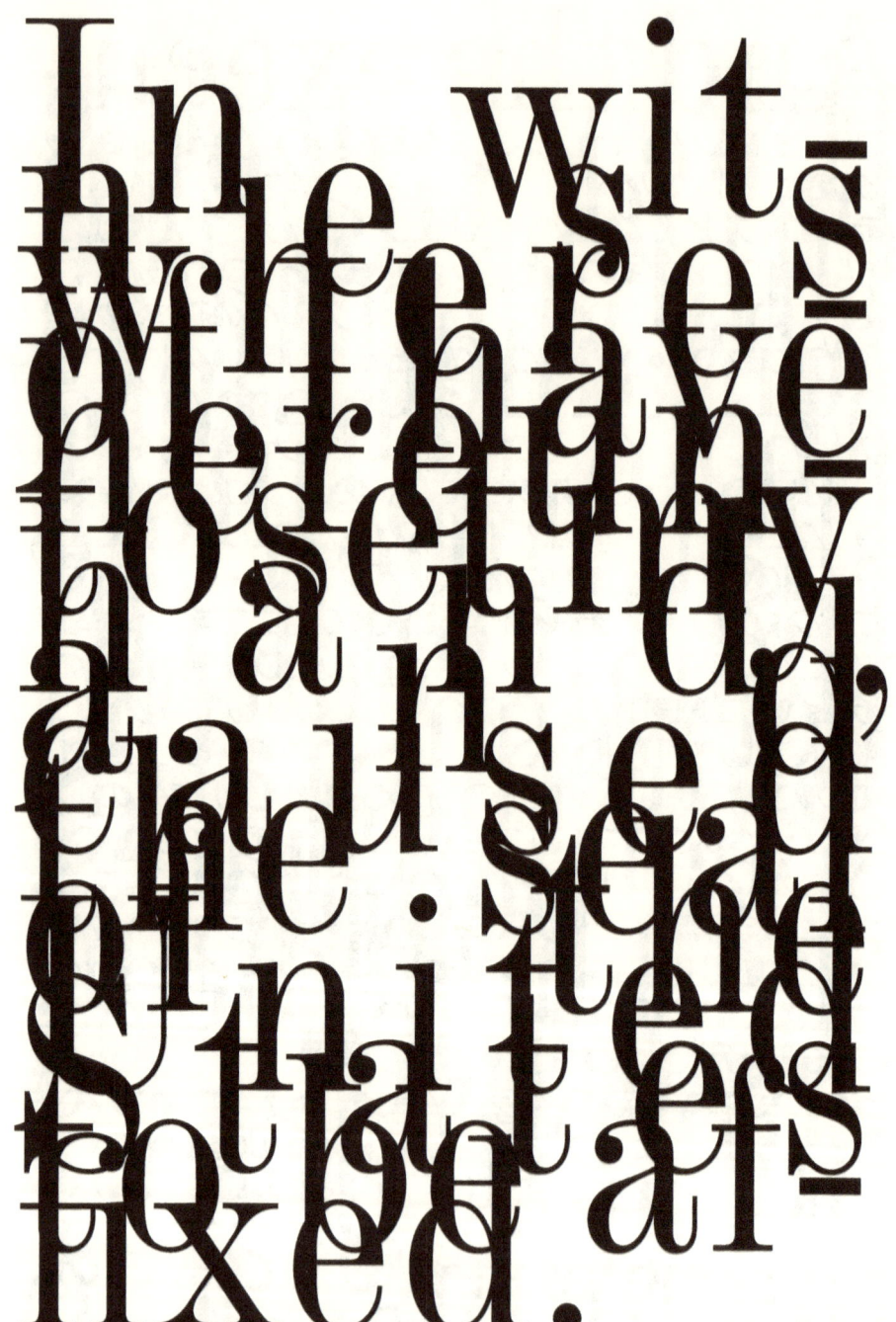

In witness whereof we have hereunto set our hand and caused the seal of the United States to be affixed.

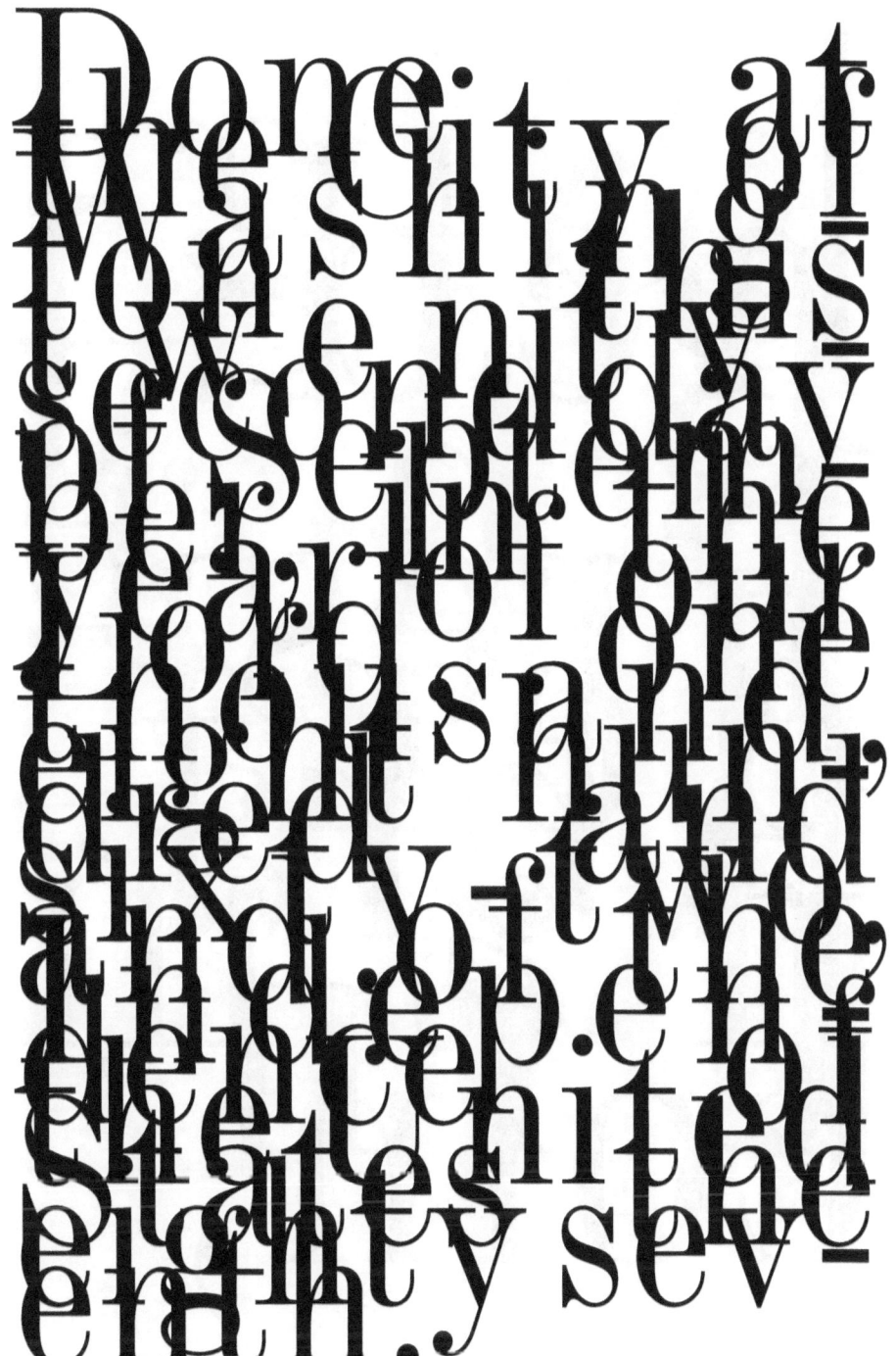

[Signed by President Abraham Lincoln,

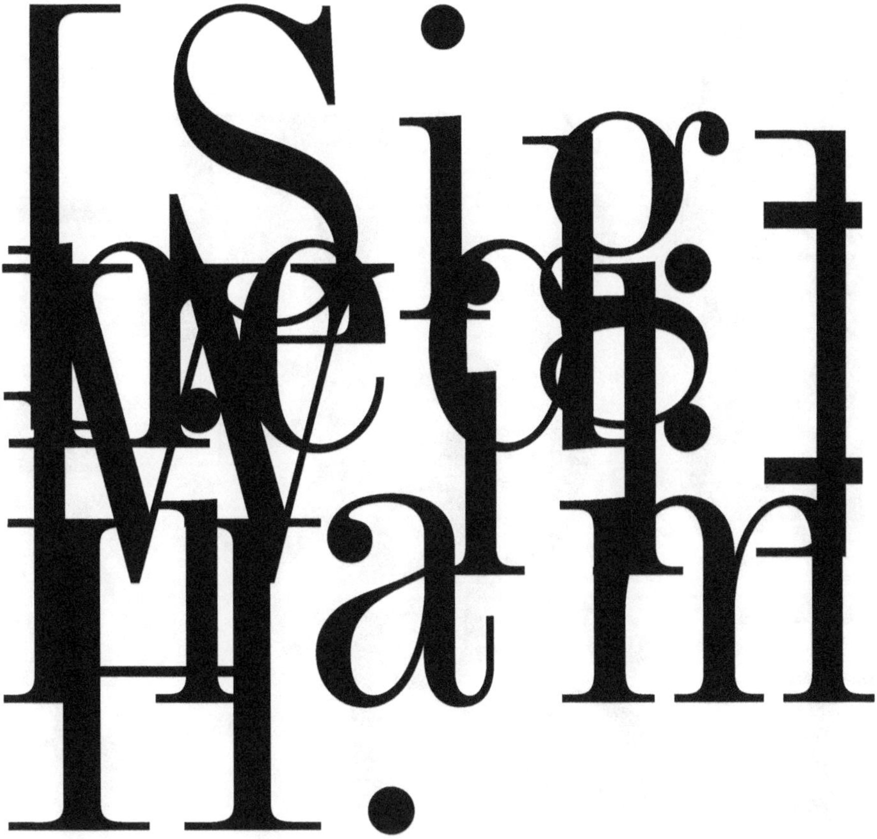

[Signature]

[of]

[Abraham]

[Lincoln]

[A. Lincoln]

Sew-,
secretary
State

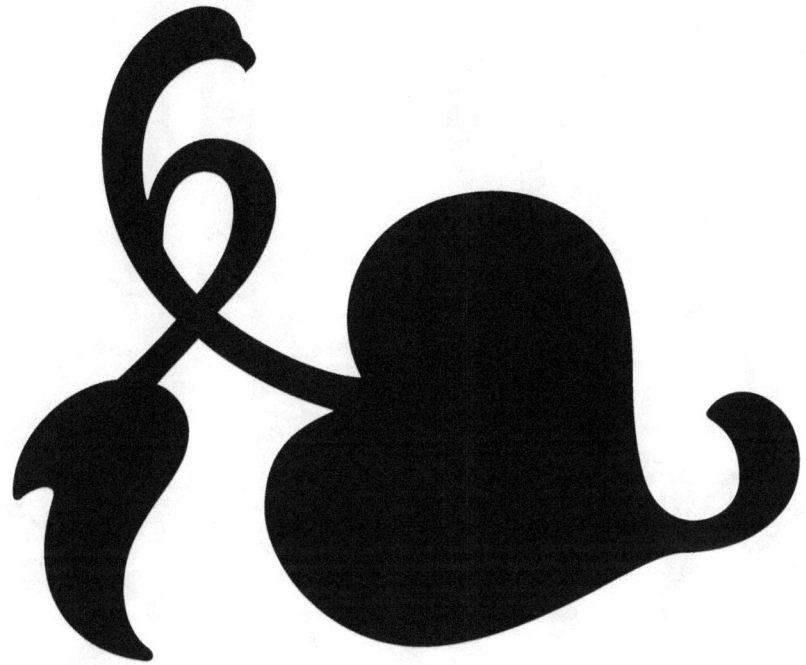

The Gettysburg Address

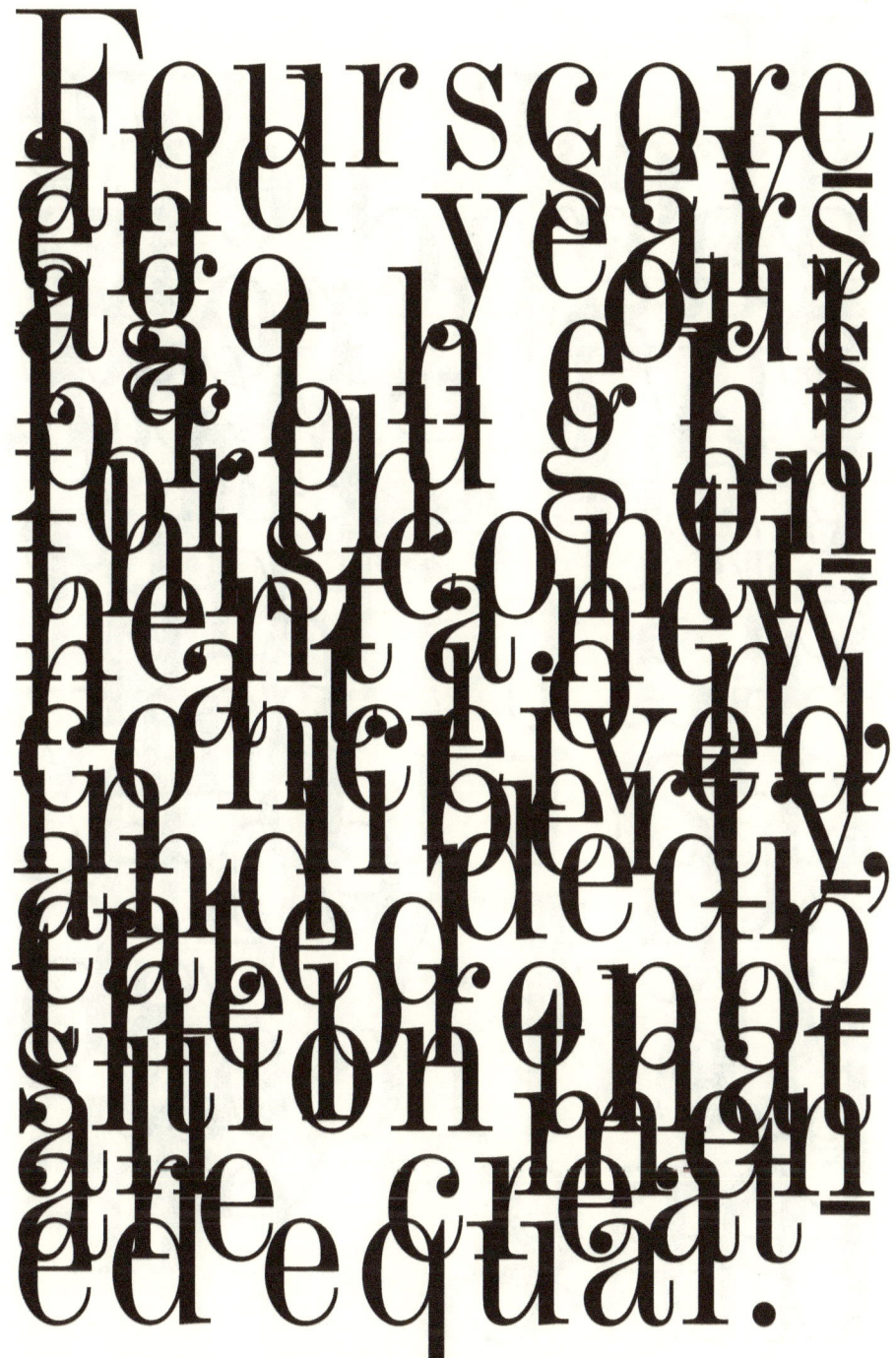

Fourscore and years ago our brought forth on this continent a new conceived in liberty and dedicated to the proposition that all men are created equal.

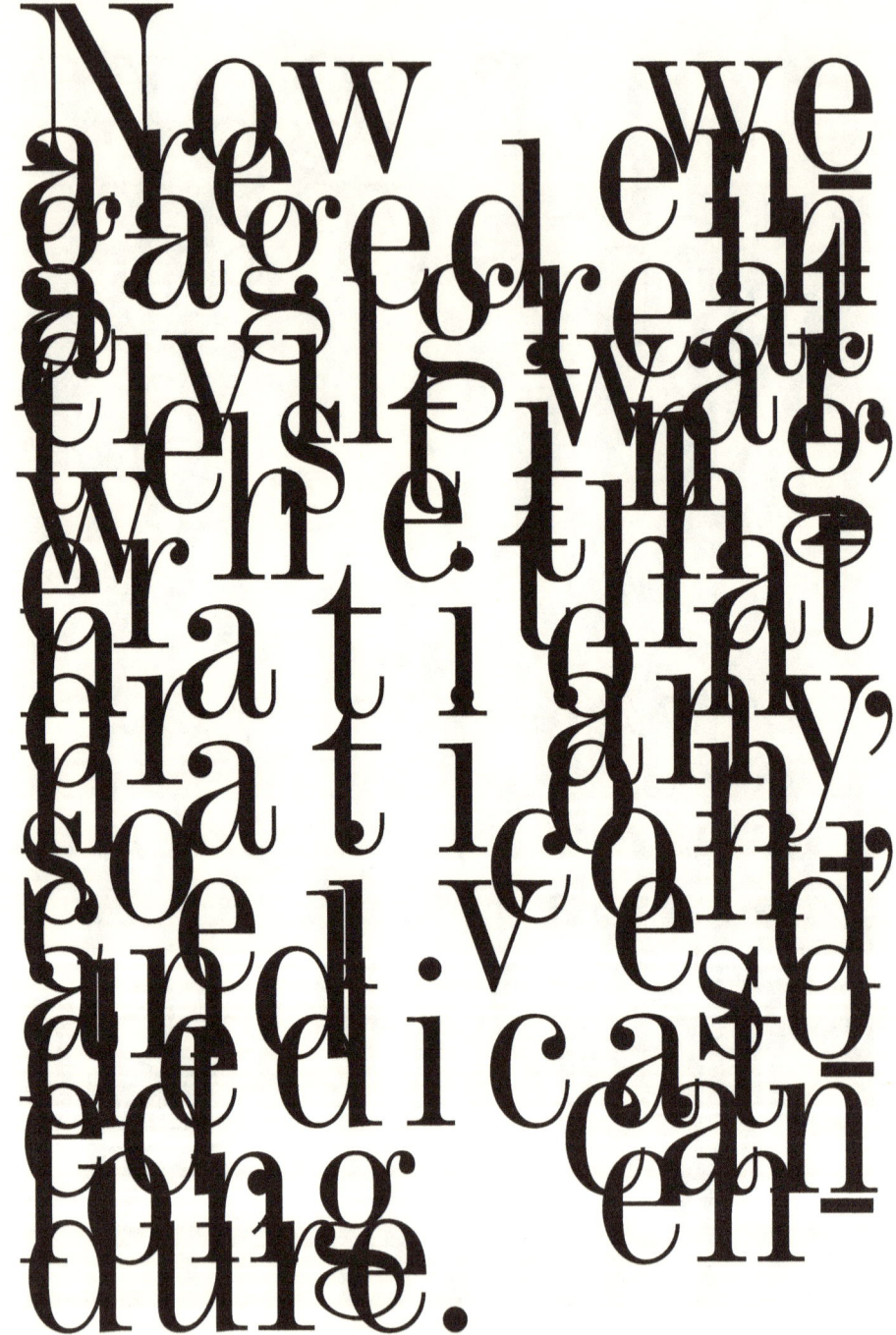

Now we are engaged in a great civil war, whether that nation, or any nation so dedicated, can endure.

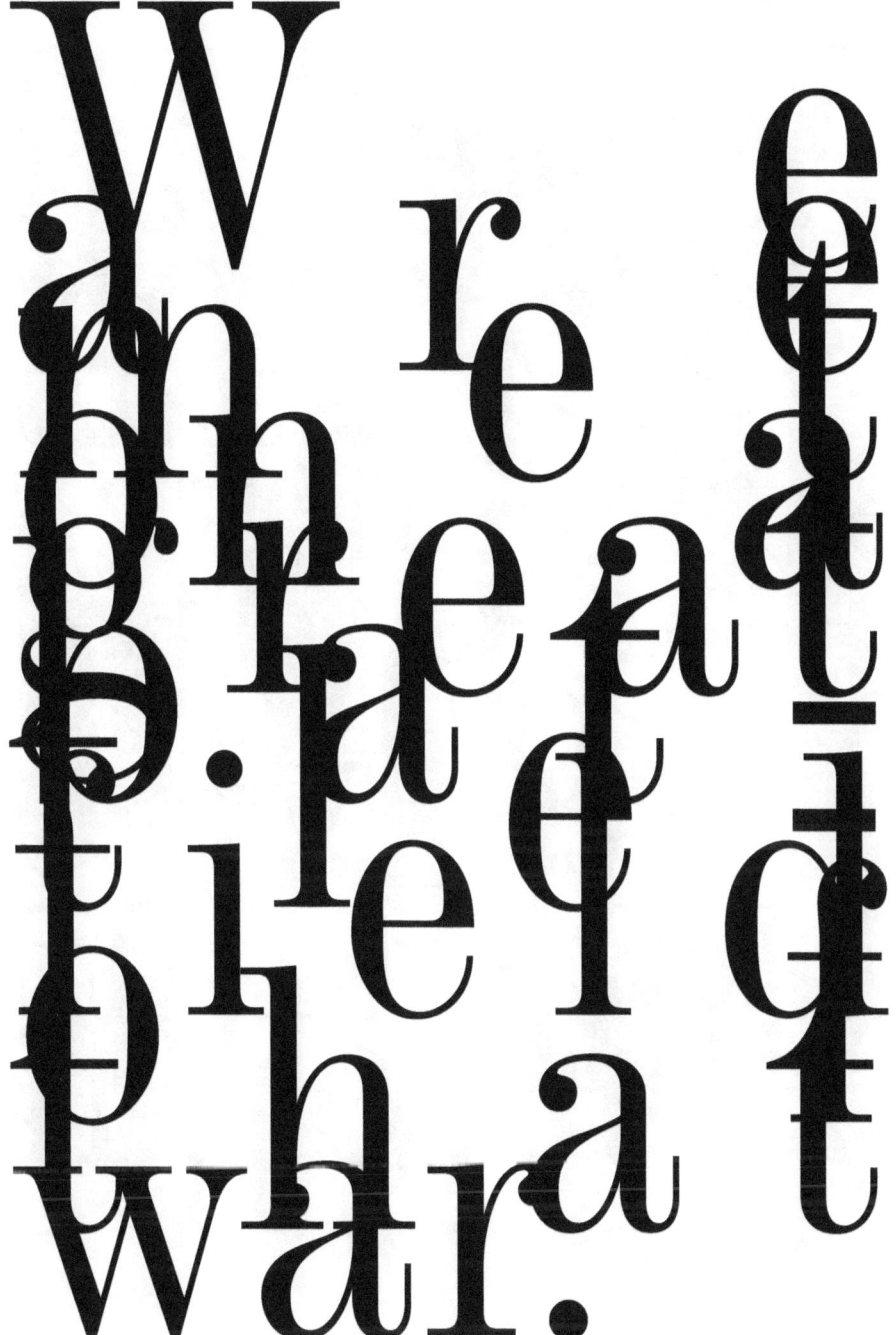

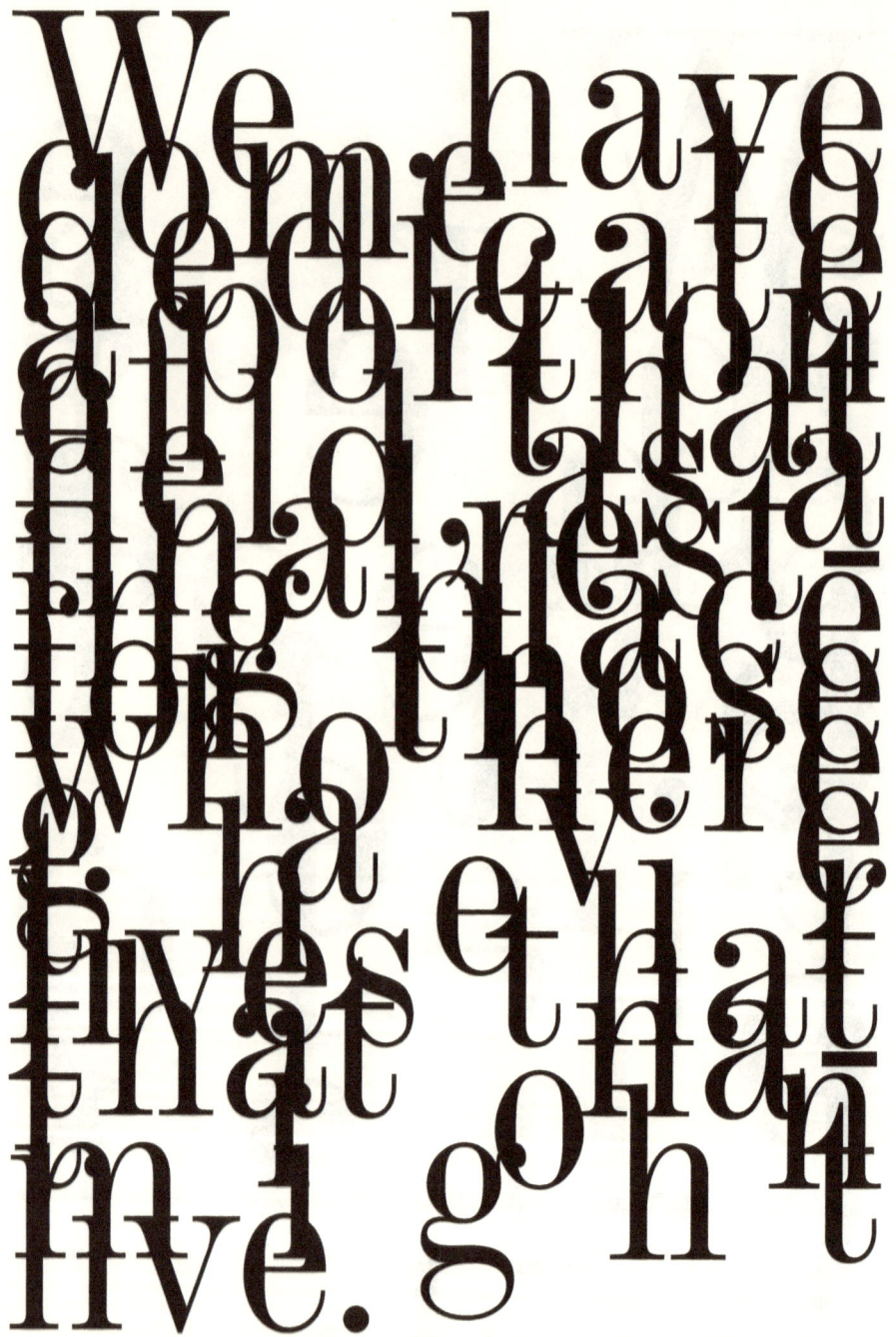

We have dedicated a portion of that field, as a final resting place for those who here gave their lives that that nation might live.

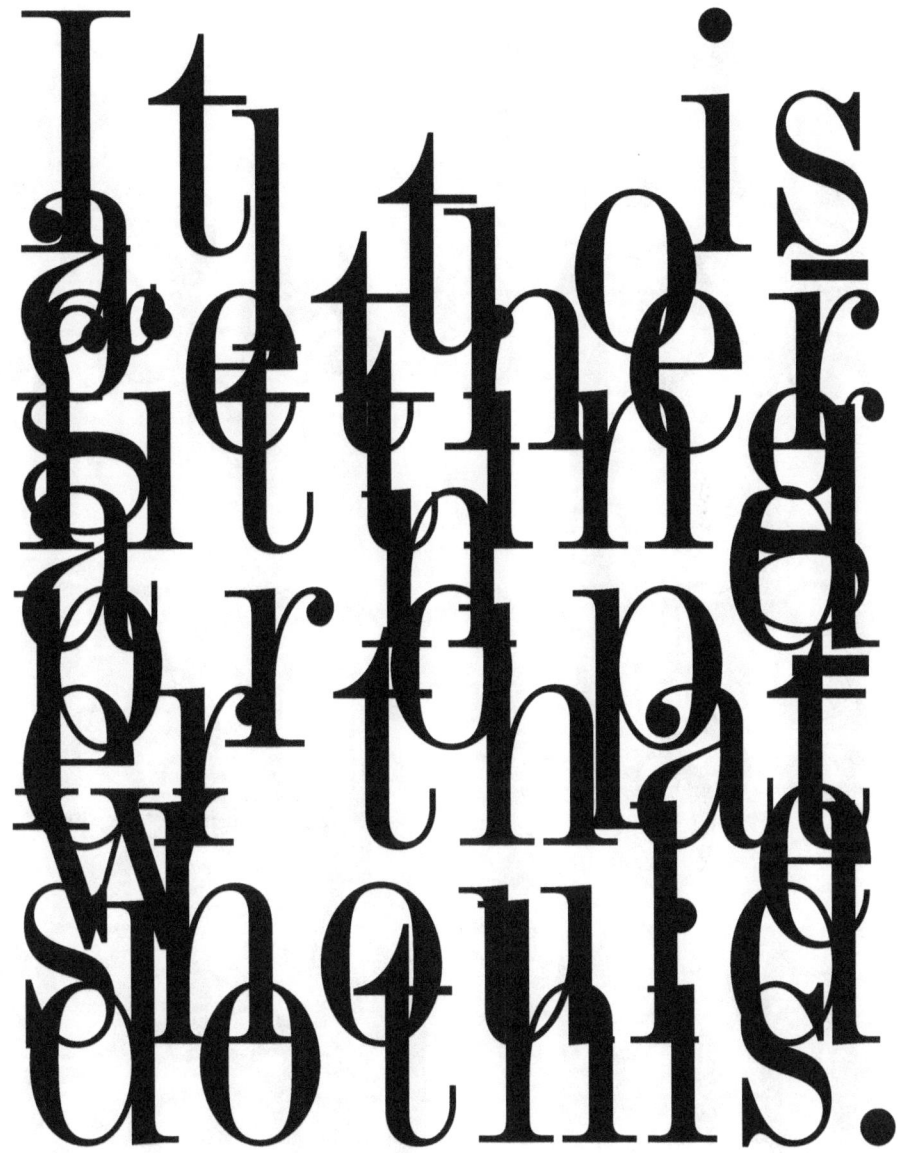

It is altogether fitting and proper that we should do this.

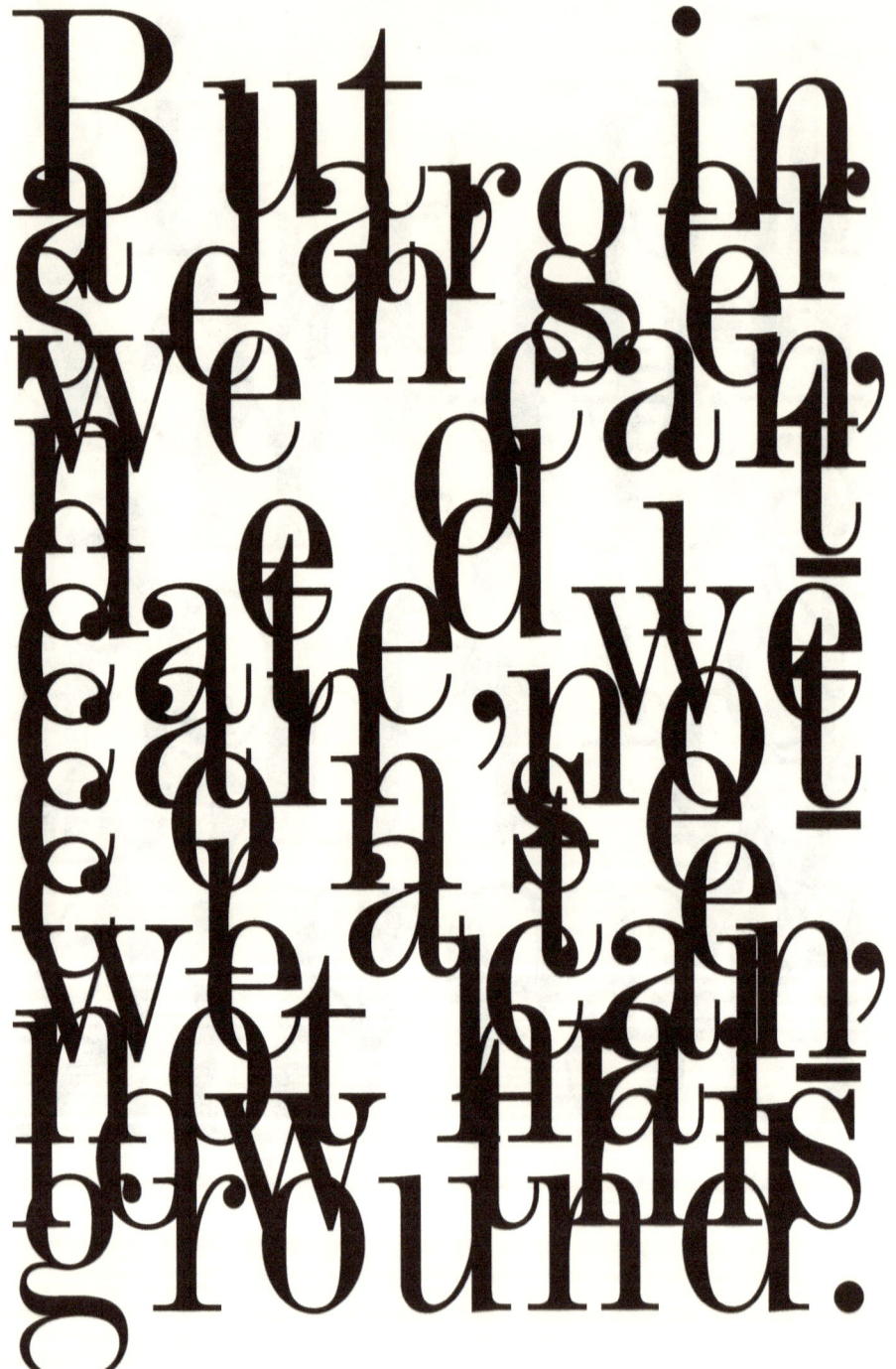

But in a larger sense, we can not dedicate, we can not consecrate, we can not hallow, this ground.

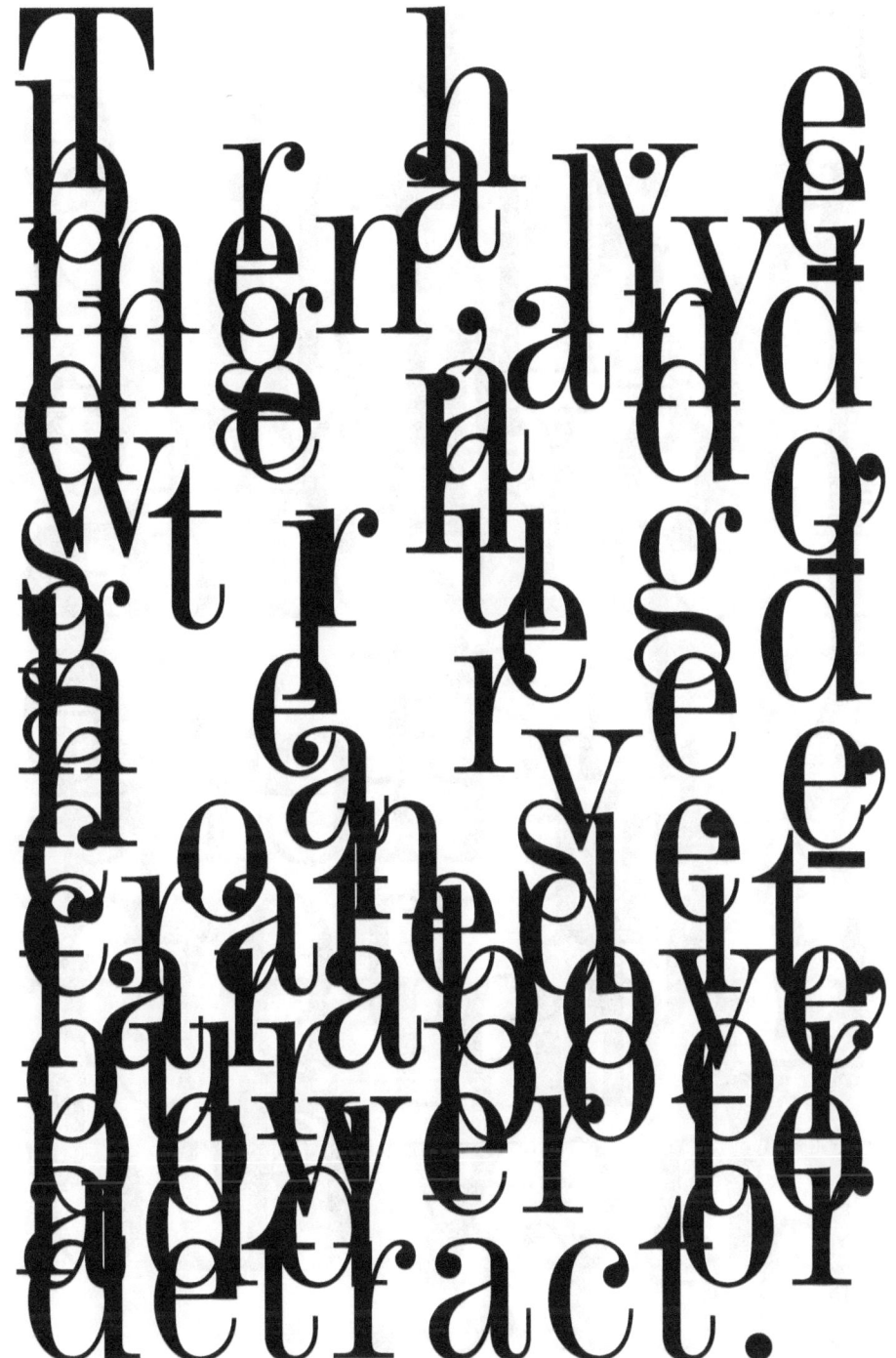

The brave men, living and dead, who struggled here, have consecrated it far above our poor power to add or detract.

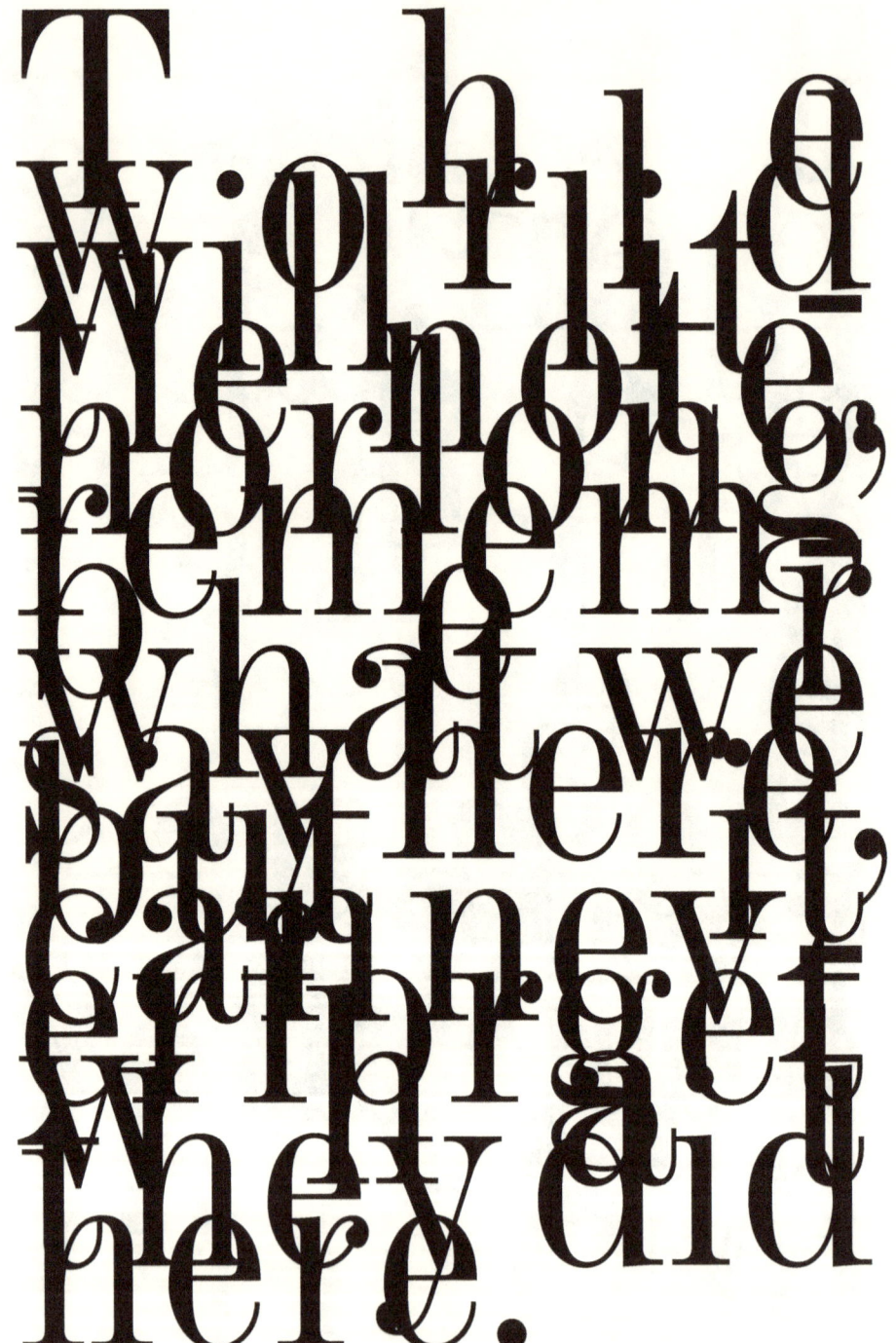

The world will little note, nor long remember, what we say here, but it can never forget what they did here.

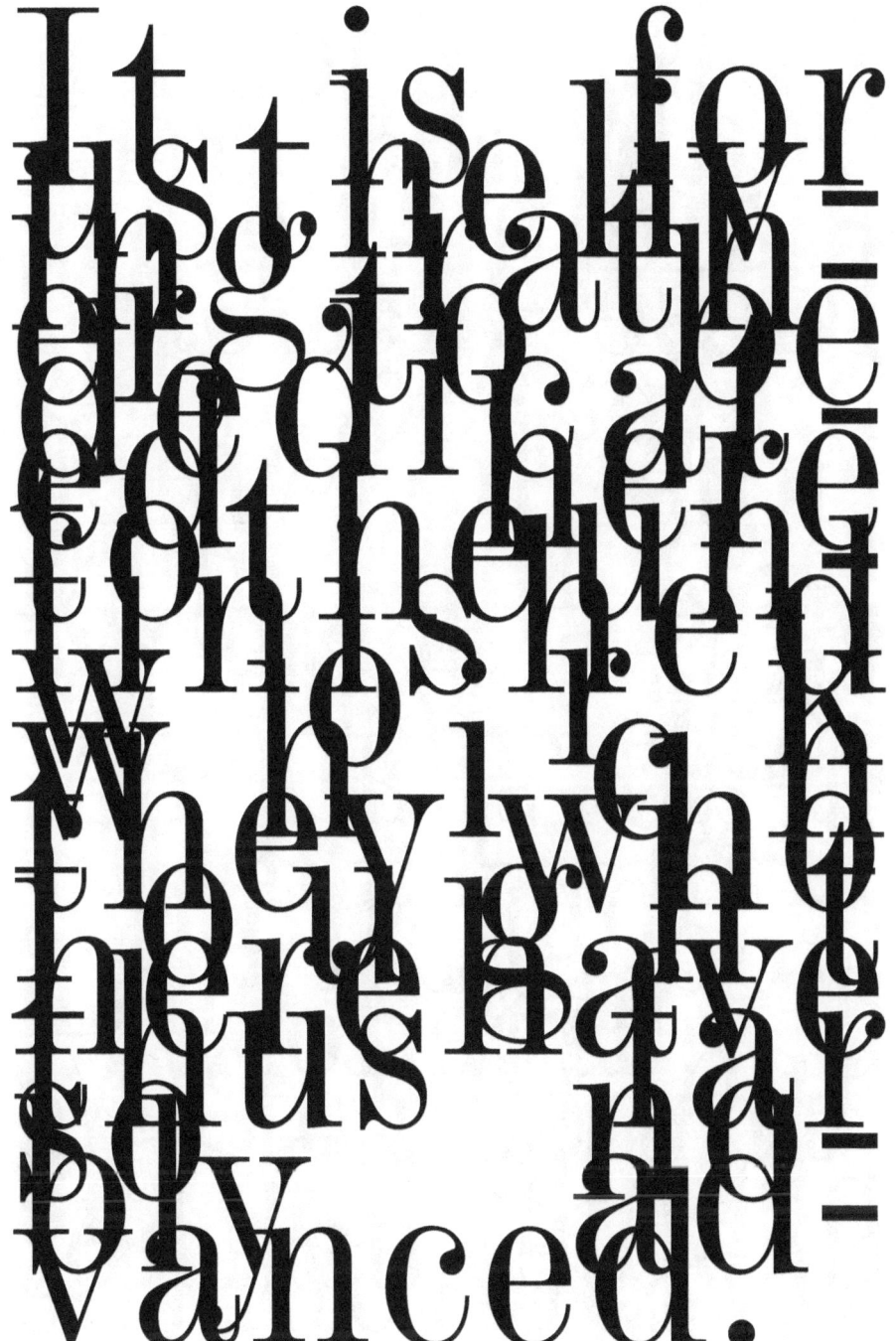

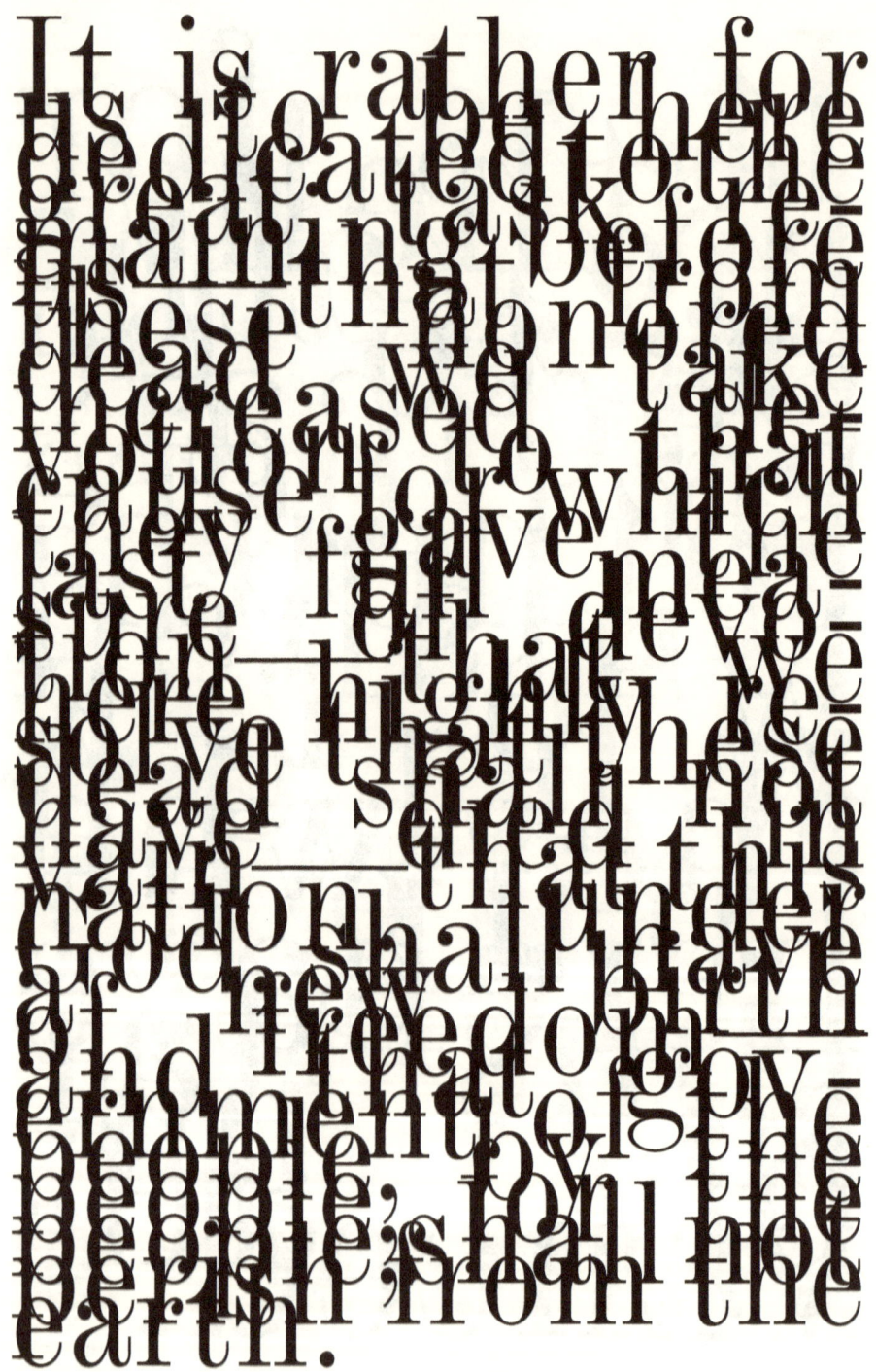

It is rather for us to be here dedicated to the great task remaining before us — that from these honored dead we take increased devotion to that cause for which they gave the last full measure of devotion — that we here highly resolve that these dead shall not have died in vain — that this nation, under God, shall have a new birth of freedom — and that government of the people, by the people, for the people, shall not perish from the earth.

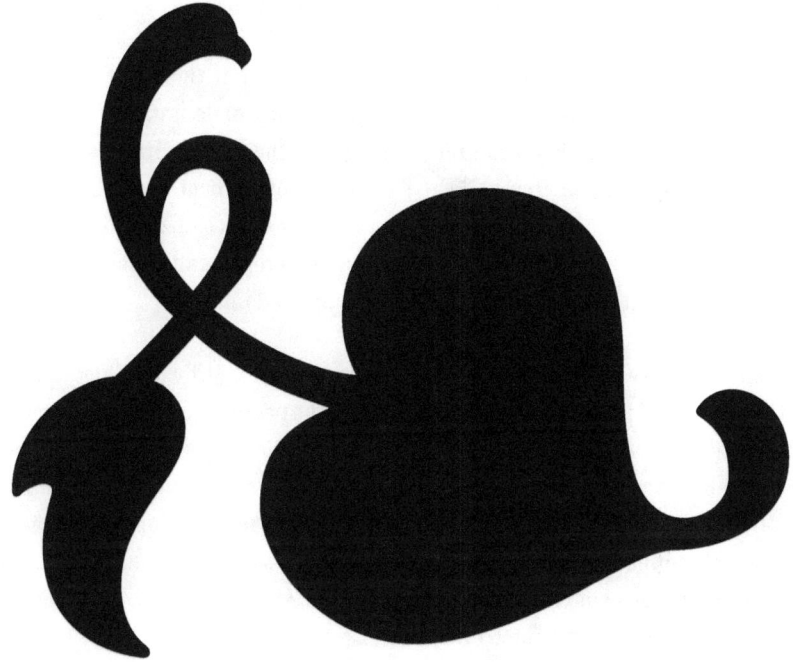

Final Version
The Emancipation Proclamation January 1, 1863 A Transcription
By the President of the United States of America:

A Proclamation.

Whereas, on the twenty-second day of September, in the year of our Lord one thousand eight hundred and sixty-two, a proclamation was issued by the President of the United States, containing, among other things, the following, to wit:

"That on the first day of January, in the year of our Lord one thousand eight hundred and sixty-three, all persons held as slaves within any State or designated part of a State, the people whereof shall then be in rebellion against the United States, shall be then, thenceforward, and forever free; and the Executive Government of the United States, including the military and naval authority thereof, will recognize and maintain the freedom of such persons, and will do no act or acts to repress such persons, or any of them, in any efforts they may make for their actual freedom."

"That the Executive will, on the first day of January aforesaid, by proclamation, designate the States and parts of States, if any, in which the people thereof, respectively, shall then be in rebellion against the United States; and the fact that any State, or the people thereof, shall on that day be, in good faith, represented in the Congress of the United States by members chosen thereto at elections wherein a majority of the qualified voters of such State shall have participated, shall, in the absence of strong countervailing testimony, be deemed conclusive evidence that such State, and the people thereof, are not then in rebellion against the United States."

Now, therefore I, Abraham Lincoln, President of the United States, by virtue of the power in me vested as Commander-in-Chief, of the Army and Navy of the United States in time of actual armed rebellion against the authority and government of the United States, and as a fit and necessary war measure for suppressing said rebellion, do, on this first day of January, in the year of our Lord one thousand eight hundred and sixty-three, and in accordance with my purpose so to do publicly proclaimed for the full period of one hundred days, from the day first above mentioned, order and designate as the States and parts of States wherein the people thereof respectively, are this day in rebellion against the United States, the following, to wit: Arkansas, Texas, Louisiana, (except the Parishes of St. Bernard, Plaquemines, Jefferson, St. John, St. Charles,

St. James Ascension, Assumption, Terrebonne, Lafourche, St. Mary, St. Martin, and Orleans, including the City of New Orleans) Mississippi, Alabama, Florida, Georgia, South Carolina, North Carolina, and Virginia, (except the forty-eight counties designated as West Virginia, and also the counties of Berkley, Accomac, Northampton, Elizabeth City, York, Princess Ann, and Norfolk, including the cities of Norfolk and Portsmouth[)], and which excepted parts, are for the present, left precisely as if this proclamation were not issued.

And by virtue of the power, and for the purpose aforesaid, I do order and declare that all persons held as slaves within said designated States, and parts of States, are, and henceforward shall be free; and that the Executive government of the United States, including the military and naval authorities thereof, will recognize and maintain the freedom of said persons.

And I hereby enjoin upon the people so declared to be free to abstain from all violence, unless in necessary self-defence; and I recommend to them that, in all cases when allowed, they labor faithfully for reasonable wages.

And I further declare and make known, that such persons of suitable condition, will be received into the armed service of the United States to garrison forts, positions, stations, and other places, and to man vessels of all sorts in said service.

And upon this act, sincerely believed to be an act of justice, warranted by the Constitution, upon military necessity, I invoke the considerate judgment of mankind, and the gracious favor of Almighty God.

In witness whereof, I have hereunto set my hand and caused the seal of the United States to be affixed.

Done at the City of Washington, this first day of January, in the year of our Lord one thousand eight hundred and sixty three, and of the Independence of the United States of America the eighty-seventh.

By the President: ABRAHAM LINCOLN

WILLIAM H. SEWARD, Secretary of State.

Preliminary Emancipation Proclamation, September 22, 1862
By the President of the United States of America.

A Proclamation.

I, Abraham Lincoln, President of the United States of America, and Commander-in-Chief of the Army and Navy thereof, do hereby proclaim and declare that hereafter, as heretofore, the war will be prosecuted for the object of practically restoring the constitutional relation between the United States, and each of the States, and the people thereof, in which States that relation is, or may be, suspended or disturbed.

That it is my purpose, upon the next meeting of Congress to again recommend the adoption of a practical measure tendering pecuniary aid to the free acceptance or rejection of all slave States, so called, the people whereof may not then be in rebellion against the United States and which States may then have voluntarily adopted, or thereafter may voluntarily adopt, immediate or gradual abolishment of slavery within their respective limits; and that the effort to colonize persons of African descent, with their consent, upon this continent, or elsewhere, with the previously obtained consent of the Governments existing there, will be continued.

That on the first day of January in the year of our Lord, one thousand eight hundred and sixty-three, all persons held as slaves within any State, or designated part of a State, the people whereof shall then be in rebellion against the United States shall be then, thenceforward, and forever free; and the executive government of the United States, including the military and naval authority thereof, will recognize and maintain the freedom of such persons, and will do no act or acts to repress such persons, or any of them, in any efforts they may make for their actual freedom.

That the executive will, on the first day of January aforesaid, by proclamation, designate the States, and part of States, if any, in which the people thereof respectively, shall then be in rebellion against the United States; and the fact that any State, or the people thereof shall, on that day be, in good faith represented in the Congress of the United States, by members chosen thereto, at elections wherein a majority of the qualified voters of such State shall have participated, shall, in the absence of strong countervailing testimony, be deemed conclusive evidence that such State and the people thereof, are not then in rebellion against the United States. That attention is hereby called to an Act of Congress entitled "An Act to make an additional Article of War" approved March

13, 1862, and which act is in the words and figure following:

"Be it enacted by the Senate and House of Representatives of the United States of America in Congress assembled, That hereafter the following shall be promulgated as an additional article of war for the government of the army of the United States, and shall be obeyed and observed as such:

"Article-All officers or persons in the military or naval service of the United States are prohibited from employing any of the forces under their respective commands for the purpose of returning fugitives from service or labor, who may have escaped from any persons to whom such service or labor is claimed to be due, and any officer who shall be found guilty by a court martial of violating this article shall be dismissed from the service.

"Sec. 2. And be it further enacted, That this act shall take effect from and after its passage."

Also to the ninth and tenth sections of an act entitled "An Act to suppress Insurrection, to punish Treason and Rebellion, to seize and confiscate property of rebels, and for other purposes," approved July 17, 1862, and which sections are in the words and figures following:

"Sec. 9. And be it further enacted, That all slaves of persons who shall hereafter be engaged in rebellion against the government of the United States, or who shall in any way give aid or comfort thereto, escaping from such persons and taking refuge within the lines of the army; and all slaves captured from such persons or deserted by them and coming under the control of the government of the United States; and all slaves of such persons found on (or) being within any place occupied by rebel forces and afterwards occupied by the forces of the United States, shall be deemed captives of war, and shall be forever free of their servitude and not again held as slaves.

"Sec. 10. And be it further enacted, That no slave escaping into any State, Territory, or the District of Columbia, from any other State, shall be delivered up, or in any way impeded or hindered of his liberty, except for crime, or some offence against the laws, unless the person claiming said fugitive shall first make oath that the person to whom the labor or service of such fugitive is alleged to be due is his lawful owner, and has not borne arms against the United States in the present rebellion, nor in any way given aid and comfort thereto; and no person engaged in the military or naval service of the United States shall, under any pretence whatever, assume to decide on the validity of the claim of any person to the service or labor of any other person, or surrender up any such person to the claimant, on pain of being dismissed from the service."

And I do hereby enjoin upon and order all persons engaged in the military and naval service of the United States to observe, obey, and enforce, within their respective spheres of service, the act, and sections above recited.

And the executive will in due time recommend that all citizens of the United States who shall have remained loyal thereto throughout the rebellion, shall (upon the restoration of the constitutional relation between the United States, and their respective States, and people, if that relation shall have been suspended or disturbed) be compensated for all losses by acts of the United States, including the loss of slaves.

In witness whereof, I have hereunto set my hand, and caused the seal of the United States to be affixed.

Done at the City of Washington this twenty-second day of September, in the year of our Lord, one thousand, eight hundred and sixty-two, and of the Independence of the United States the eighty seventh.

[Signed:] By the President, Abraham Lincoln,

[Signed:] William H. Seward, Secretary of State

The Gettysburg Address

Four score and seven years ago our fathers brought forth on this continent a new nation, conceived in liberty, and dedicated to the proposition that all men are created equal.

Now we are engaged in a great civil war, testing whether that nation, or any nation, so conceived and so dedicated, can long endure.

We are met on a great battle-field of that war.

We have come to dedicate a portion of that field, as a final resting place for those who here gave their lives that that nation might live.

It is altogether fitting and proper that we should do this.

But, in a larger sense, we can not dedicate, we can not consecrate, we can not hallow this ground.

The brave men, living and dead, who struggled here, have consecrated it, far above our poor power to add or detract.

The world will little note, nor long remember what we say here, but it can never forget what they did here.

It is for us the living, rather, to be dedicated here to the unfinished work which they who fought here have thus far so nobly advanced.

It is rather for us to be here dedicated to the great task remaining before us—that from these honored dead we take increased devotion to that cause for which they gave the last full measure of devotion—that we here highly resolve that these dead shall not have died in vain   that this nation, under God, shall have a new birth of freedom—and that government of the people, by the people, for the people, shall not perish from the earth.

﹏

1	0.262777559	38	9.985547234	75	19.70831691
2	0.525555118	39	10.24832479	76	19.97109447
3	0.788332676	40	10.51110235	77	20.23387203
4	1.051110235	41	10.77387991	78	20.49664959
5	1.313887794	42	11.03665747	79	20.75942714
6	1.576665353	43	11.29943503	80	21.0222047
7	1.839442912	44	11.56221259	81	21.28498226
8	2.10222047	45	11.82499015	82	21.54775982
9	2.364998029	46	12.0877677	83	21.81053738
10	2.627775588	47	12.35054526	84	22.07331494
11	2.890553147	48	12.61332282	85	22.3360925
12	3.153330706	49	12.87610038	86	22.59887006
13	3.416108264	50	13.13887794	87	22.86164762
14	3.678885823	51	13.4016555	88	23.12442517
15	3.941663382	52	13.66443306	89	23.38720273
16	4.204440941	53	13.92721062	90	23.64998029
17	4.4672185	54	14.18998818	91	23.91275785
18	4.729996058	55	14.45276573	92	24.17553541
19	4.992773617	56	14.71554329	93	24.43831297
20	5.255551176	57	14.97832085	94	24.70109053
21	5.518328735	58	15.24109841	95	24.96386809
22	5.781106294	59	15.50387597	96	25.22664564
23	6.043883852	60	15.76665353	97	25.4894232
24	6.306661411	61	16.02943109	98	25.75220076
25	6.56943897	62	16.29220865	99	26.01497832
26	6.832216529	63	16.5549862	100	26.27775588
27	7.094994088	64	16.81776376	101	26.54053344
28	7.357771646	65	17.08054132	102	26.803311
29	7.620549205	66	17.34331888	103	27.06608856
30	7.883326764	67	17.60609644	104	27.32886611
31	8.146104323	68	17.868874	105	27.59164367
32	8.408881881	69	18.13165156	106	27.85442123
33	8.67165944	70	18.39442912	107	28.11719879
34	8.934436999	71	18.65720667	108	28.37997635
35	9.197214558	72	18.91998423	109	28.64275391
36	9.459992117	73	19.18276179	110	28.90553147
37	9.722769675	74	19.44553935	111	29.16830903

112	29.43108659	149	39.15385626	186	48.87662594
113	29.69386414	150	39.41663382	187	49.13940349
114	29.9566417	151	39.67941138	188	49.40218105
115	30.21941926	152	39.94218894	189	49.66495861
116	30.48219682	153	40.2049665	190	49.92773617
117	30.74497438	154	40.46774405	191	50.19051373
118	31.00775194	155	40.73052161	192	50.45329129
119	31.2705295	156	40.99329917	193	50.71606885
120	31.53330706	157	41.25607673	194	50.97884641
121	31.79608461	158	41.51885429	195	51.24162397
122	32.05886217	159	41.78163185	196	51.50440152
123	32.32163973	160	42.04440941	197	51.76717908
124	32.58441729	161	42.30718697	198	52.02995664
125	32.84719485	162	42.56996453	199	52.2927342
126	33.10997241	163	42.83274208	200	52.55551176
127	33.37274997	164	43.09551964	201	52.81828932
128	33.63552753	165	43.3582972	202	53.08106688
129	33.89830508	166	43.62107476	203	53.34384444
130	34.16108264	167	43.88385232	204	53.60662199
131	34.4238602	168	44.14662988	205	53.86939955
132	34.68663776	169	44.40940744	206	54.13217711
133	34.94941532	170	44.672185	207	54.39495467
134	35.21219288	171	44.93496255	208	54.65773223
135	35.47497044	172	45.19774011	209	54.92050979
136	35.737748	173	45.46051767	210	55.18328735
137	36.00052556	174	45.72329523	211	55.44606491
138	36.26330311	175	45.98607279	212	55.70884246
139	36.52608067	176	46.24885035	213	55.97162002
140	36.78885823	177	46.51162791	214	56.23439758
141	37.05163579	178	46.77440547	215	56.49717514
142	37.31441335	179	47.03718302	216	56.7599527
143	37.57719091	180	47.29996058	217	57.02273026
144	37.83996847	181	47.56273814	218	57.28550782
145	38.10274603	182	47.8255157	219	57.54828538
146	38.36552358	183	48.08829326	220	57.81106294
147	38.62830114	184	48.35107082	221	58.07384049
148	38.8910787	185	48.61384838	222	58.33661805

223	58.59939561	260	68.32216529	297	78.04493496
224	58.86217317	261	68.58494285	298	78.30771252
225	59.12495073	262	68.8477204	299	78.57049008
226	59.38772829	263	69.11049796	300	78.83326764
227	59.65050585	264	69.37327552	301	79.0960452
228	59.91328341	265	69.63605308	302	79.35882276
229	60.17606096	266	69.89883064	303	79.62160032
230	60.43883852	267	70.1616082	304	79.88437787
231	60.70161608	268	70.42438576	305	80.14715543
232	60.96439364	269	70.68716332	306	80.40993299
233	61.2271712	270	70.94994088	307	80.67271055
234	61.48994876	271	71.21271843	308	80.93548811
235	61.75272632	272	71.47549599	309	81.19826567
236	62.01550388	273	71.73827355	310	81.46104323
237	62.27828143	274	72.00105111	311	81.72382079
238	62.54105899	275	72.26382867	312	81.98659834
239	62.80383655	276	72.52660623	313	82.2493759
240	63.06661411	277	72.78938379	314	82.51215346
241	63.32939167	278	73.05216135	315	82.77493102
242	63.59216923	279	73.3149389	316	83.03770858
243	63.85494679	280	73.57771646	317	83.30048614
244	64.11772435	281	73.84049402	318	83.5632637
245	64.38050191	282	74.10327158	319	83.82604126
246	64.64327946	283	74.36604914	320	84.08881881
247	64.90605702	284	74.6288267	321	84.35159637
248	65.16883458	285	74.89160426	322	84.61437393
249	65.43161214	286	75.15438182	323	84.87715149
250	65.6943897	287	75.41715937	324	85.13992905
251	65.95716726	288	75.67993693	325	85.40270661
252	66.21994482	289	75.94271449	326	85.66548417
253	66.48272238	290	76.20549205	327	85.92826173
254	66.74549993	291	76.46826961	328	86.19103929
255	67.00827749	292	76.73104717	329	86.45381684
256	67.27105505	293	76.99382473	330	86.7165944
257	67.53383261	294	77.25660229	331	86.97937196
258	67.79661017	295	77.51937984	332	87.24214952
259	68.05938773	296	77.7821574	333	87.50492708

334	87.76770464	371	97.49047431	408	107.213244
335	88.0304822	372	97.75325187	409	107.4760215
336	88.29325976	373	98.01602943	410	107.7387991
337	88.55603731	374	98.27880699	411	108.0015767
338	88.81881487	375	98.54158455	412	108.2643542
339	89.08159243	376	98.80436211	413	108.5271318
340	89.34436999	377	99.06713967	414	108.7899093
341	89.60714755	378	99.32991723	415	109.0526869
342	89.86992511	379	99.59269478	416	109.3154645
343	90.13270267	380	99.85547234	417	109.578242
344	90.39548023	381	100.1182499	418	109.8410196
345	90.65825778	382	100.3810275	419	110.1037971
346	90.92103534	383	100.643805	420	110.3665747
347	91.1838129	384	100.9065826	421	110.6293523
348	91.44659046	385	101.1693601	422	110.8921298
349	91.70936802	386	101.4321377	423	111.1549074
350	91.97214558	387	101.6949153	424	111.4176849
351	92.23492314	388	101.9576928	425	111.6804625
352	92.4977007	389	102.2204704	426	111.94324
353	92.76047826	390	102.4832479	427	112.2060176
354	93.02325581	391	102.7460255	428	112.4687952
355	93.28603337	392	103.008803	429	112.7315727
356	93.54881093	393	103.2715806	430	112.9943503
357	93.81158849	394	103.5343582	431	113.2571278
358	94.07436605	395	103.7971357	432	113.5199054
359	94.33714361	396	104.0599133	433	113.782683
360	94.59992117	397	104.3226908	434	114.0454605
361	94.86269873	398	104.5854684	435	114.3082381
362	95.12547628	399	104.848246	436	114.5710156
363	95.38825384	400	105.1110235	437	114.8337932
364	95.6510314	401	105.3738011	438	115.0965708
365	95.91380896	402	105.6365786	439	115.3593483
366	96.17658652	403	105.8993562	440	115.6221259
367	96.43936408	404	106.1621338	441	115.8849034
368	96.70214164	405	106.4249113	442	116.147681
369	96.9649192	406	106.6876889	443	116.4104585
370	97.22769675	407	106.9504664	444	116.6732361

445	116.9360137	482	126.6587833	519	136.381553
446	117.1987912	483	126.9215609	520	136.6443306
447	117.4615688	484	127.1843385	521	136.9071081
448	117.7243463	485	127.447116	522	137.1698857
449	117.9871239	486	127.7098936	523	137.4326633
450	118.2499015	487	127.9726711	524	137.6954408
451	118.512679	488	128.2354487	525	137.9582184
452	118.7754566	489	128.4982263	526	138.2209959
453	119.0382341	490	128.7610038	527	138.4837735
454	119.3010117	491	129.0237814	528	138.746551
455	119.5637893	492	129.2865589	529	139.0093286
456	119.8265668	493	129.5493365	530	139.2721062
457	120.0893444	494	129.812114	531	139.5348837
458	120.3521219	495	130.0748916	532	139.7976613
459	120.6148995	496	130.3376692	533	140.0604388
460	120.877677	497	130.6004467	534	140.3232164
461	121.1404546	498	130.8632243	535	140.585994
462	121.4032322	499	131.1260018	536	140.8487715
463	121.6660097	500	131.3887794	537	141.1115491
464	121.9287873	501	131.651557	538	141.3743266
465	122.1915648	502	131.9143345	539	141.6371042
466	122.4543424	503	132.1771121	540	141.8998818
467	122.71712	504	132.4398896	541	142.1626593
468	122.9798975	505	132.7026672	542	142.4254369
469	123.2426751	506	132.9654448	543	142.6882144
470	123.5054526	507	133.2282223	544	142.950992
471	123.7682302	508	133.4909999	545	143.2137695
472	124.0310078	509	133.7537774	546	143.4765471
473	124.2937853	510	134.016555	547	143.7393247
474	124.5565629	511	134.2793325	548	144.0021022
475	124.8193404	512	134.5421101	549	144.2648798
476	125.082118	513	134.8048877	550	144.5276573
477	125.3448955	514	135.0676652	551	144.7904349
478	125.6076731	515	135.3304428	552	145.0532125
479	125.8704507	516	135.5932203	553	145.31599
480	126.1332282	517	135.8559979	554	145.5787676
481	126.3960058	518	136.1187755	555	145.8415451

556	146.1043227
557	146.3671002
558	146.6298778
559	146.8926554
560	147.1554329
561	147.4182105
562	147.680988
563	147.9437656
564	148.2065432
565	148.4693207
566	148.7320983
567	148.9948758
568	149.2576534
569	149.520431
570	149.7832085
571	150.0459861
572	150.3087636
573	150.5715412
574	150.8343187
575	151.0970963
576	151.3598739
577	151.6226514
578	151.885429
579	152.1482065
580	152.4109841
581	152.6737617
582	152.9365392
583	153.1993168
584	153.4620943
585	153.7248719
586	153.9876495
587	154.250427
588	154.5132046
589	154.7759821
590	155.0387597

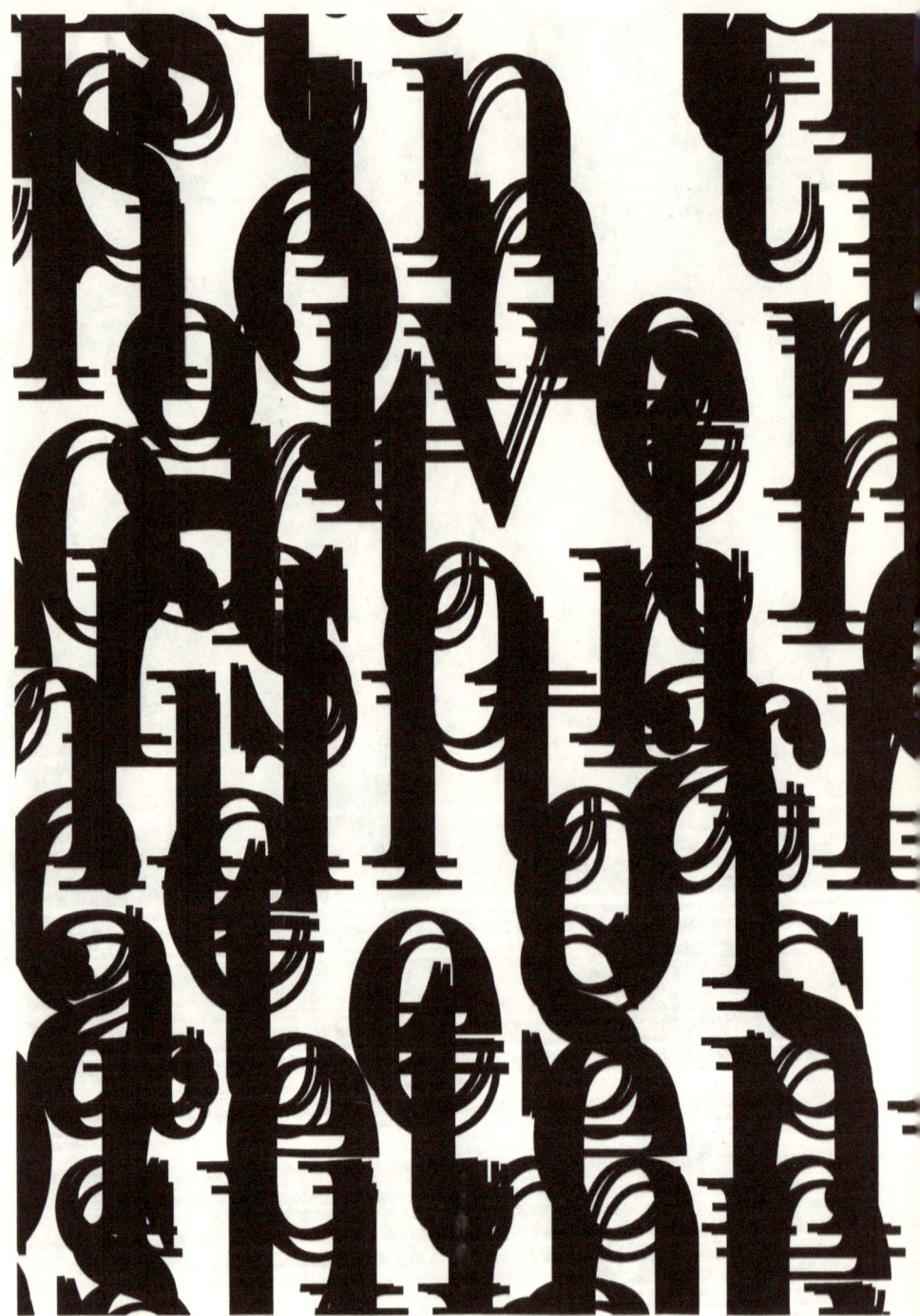

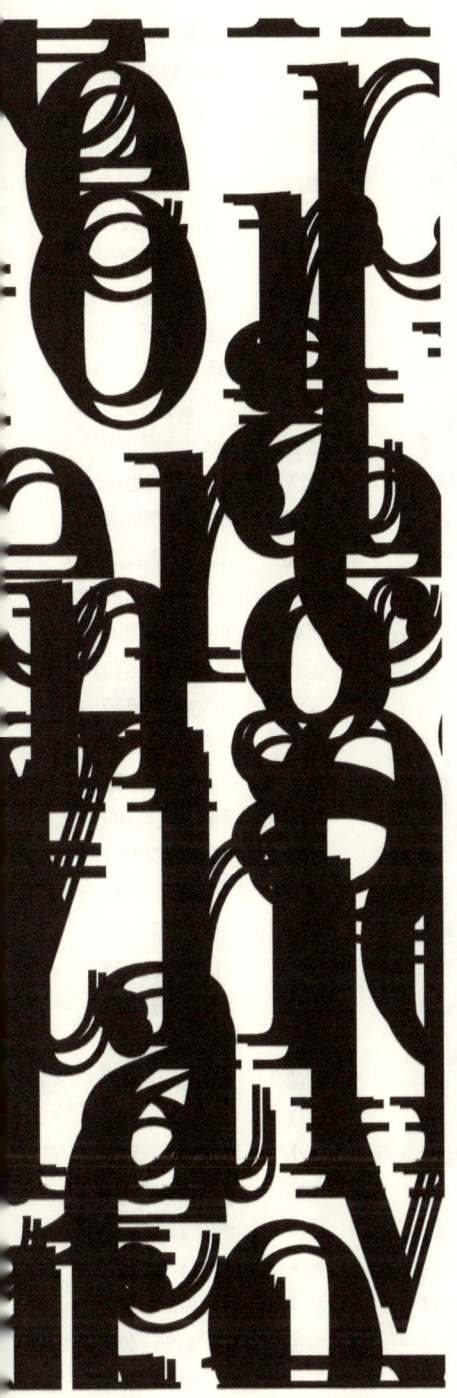

ABRAHAM LINCOLN was the 16th President of the United States, serving from March 1861 until his assassination in April of 1865. That's it. If you want more of a biography why not read a real book, like Doris Kearns Goodwin's tome, or if you're not the bookish type— you poor, poor, semi-literate dolt—then head on over to Netflix and get a look at Spielberg's take on the man from that very same book by Ms. Goodwin? Or read the one and watch the other? Then, perhaps, you can not only get some facts thrown at you about the dear man, our Lincoln, you can also bore people at cocktail parties about how Spielberg got it wrong, or right, depending on your point of view. If, after spending some quality time with the book and then another bit of another evening with the flick, you still don't have a point of view about the adaptation by Mr. Spielberg, then, possibly, you are not the kind of person to be inquisitive enough to figure out the why of the numbers that start on page eighty-five and then try, even a teensy-weensy bit, to deduce what they have in connection with the whole of a book seemingly type-set in a wrong and haphazard manner.

DAVID GREENBERG has that kind of name and affable nature which causes him to be mistaken for others sharing that moniker, as well as one—also creative by the fist-full— Greenberger: the singular David Greenberger, naturally. With so many Greenbergs named David out there, you will be summarily confused if you go on the web and try to figure out exactly which one is the only one who could have had the dim idea for crafting this esoteric book of unreadable art and then spent evenings working on it with a fervor that could seem sadly misplaced—especially when you really take a good look at the vast difference found in the chasm between hard work and that elusive "making a profit," especially the measly profit obtained by struggling artists, underscored, make that a double underscored, by the fact most works of art don't sell shit as that oft-doppelganger with a slightly larger name, and definitely larger audience, David Greenberger, knows all too well. On those lost evenings this Greenberg (no "e-r") could have been dealing with larger and more profound issues of creativity, like writing film scripts that agents, if he had some, could sell for stupid ly large amount of money, or ditching creativity altogether he could have wound up working at the Apple Store—which is more likely than the filmic pipe-dream he fantasizes about on especially dark days—where Greenberg could help customers while he, and they, both salivate over the new items that they shouldn't be coveting for two basic, and quite good, reasons. One is the exorbidant price, the other is the fact those articles were made by poorly-paid laborers over in Communist China; a country which, with the label "communist," should be looking out for the laborers, one would think. (What would Trotsky do? Marx, Lenin?) Even with some guilt darkening the goods, Greenberg could use the extra cash from moonlighting, expanded with the buying power of the employee discount to buy the family a new Apple laptop with a larger screen, and of course, help a few more Foxconn laborers send some money back home; for you see helping to burnish that guilt, just a bit for Greenberg, is the idea that this materialism could be a good thing for the brand of Communism being ladled out in China. Since without the purchases being made at Apple, those factories would send same said laborers back to the hinterland farms to starve most likely while the kleptocrats live the large life with their new iMacs all aglowing with the politically correct, for them, screensavers announcing the latest slogan to keep the countryside in the right mindset. Right now Greenberg has to squint at his dinky screen while designing projects such as this and has been for the last couple of years on many more projects so unlike this; not that he is complaining as his failing eyesight has pushed him to buy a great pair of Warby Parkers. If he sells a bunch of these books, or you get your friends to buy a few more, those dollars will be saved for another stunning pair. Maybe even splurging on some shades of the prescription persuasion with some dollars left over for that rainy day when the present laptop explodes and Greenberg has to sheepishly find his way over to the Apple Store and buy—without the discount he could have had if he was a bit more pragmatic—a new, now more expensive, laptop with that much larger screen; unless he gets distracted by something else while there, which often happens as can be testified by his children and wife. By the way, Greenberg's eye-strain during his late-night sessions in front of a tiny, darkening screen, by the old age of the laptop and maybe Greenberg's, is NOT why the book is type-set all wrong. In fact, the book is totally correct. It was designed that way with the intent, artistic you might say, to be as abstruse as Greenberg wanted it to be. It is you, you dolt, who are wrong. And by the way, kick that affable label good-bye. Kick it. Now! Greenberg is sick of sharing his Google search with so many others. Maybe he will rise to the top of that list, even nab a Wikipedia page? Of his own, chock-full of all the correct facts, with not a Greenberger in sight? Wearing his new dark Warby Parker shades perhaps Greenberg will obtain the swagger to go on with his new found confidence after kicking his affability way off-screen and out-of-sight? If history is to be any guide then that's a "nope" on the swagger and you can count the hours, nay minutes, pudgy Master Affability could stand being hidden away before showing his cute dimples once again.

A. Lincoln

3.8055

[product]

www.ingramcontent.com/pod-product-compliance
Lightning Source LLC
Chambersburg PA
CBHW022023170526
45157CB00003B/1331